WHAT IF ~~GOD'S~~
A CHRISTIAN?

?

AND OTHER THOUGHTS FROM
THE SCEPTIC BLOG

AN ORTHODOX BUT SCEPTICAL
JEWISH VIEW OF THE WORLD

By Daniel Greenberg

September 2017

Grosvenor House
Publishing Limited

This book is published by
Grosvenor House Publishing Ltd
Link House
140 The Broadway, Tolworth, Surrey, KT6 7HT.
www.grosvenorhousepublishing.co.uk

A CIP record for this book
is available from the British Library

ISBN 978-1-78623-978-5

CONTENTS

The Jewish Year

Law and Order

Jewish Community

Jewish thought

Israel

General religious issues

Environment

Charities

General society Issues

BUSINESS ETHICS ARTICLES

GLOSSARY

PREFACE

Blogging is a wonderful invention, for which wives and newspaper editors around the world are profoundly grateful.

People like me who were born with the impression that other people are likely to be interested in our views of the world, an impression which no amount of discouragement or indifference can shake, were once doomed to inflict our thoughts daily on our wives and to embody our ideas in persistent, confident and strident – but generally one-directional – correspondence with the newspapers. Now we can spare the feelings of our wives and the waste-paper baskets of Fleet Street by producing a few indignant electronic dots and scattering them to a world which – in our imagination – is eagerly waiting to read them.

The only fly in the ointment is electronic visit-counters which try, as ruthlessly as our wives and the newspaper editors once did, to disabuse us of the delusion that anybody is particularly interested in our thoughts. But it would take more than a jumped-up electronic counter ruthlessly recording lack of activity to discourage me.

So here, in response to a complete lack of public demand, is the collected edition of my electronic thoughts of the last few years. It would clearly make an ideal Chanukah / Christmas / Eid / Ramadan / Diwali / birthday / anniversary present for anyone you really dislike.

(Some of the posts have been altered because I wish I'd originally said something different.)

Organised religion of all kinds does infinitely more harm than good world-wide: it encourages and foments division and it colludes or supports wrong-doing of almost every kind. Religion is arguably the world's most significant problem today. But those of us for whom religion is important would like it to be part of the solution. This book is an attempt to demonstrate how a religious perspective can contribute usefully to the world and provide thoughts that other religions, and people who don't believe in any religion, can find useful.

I have also reprinted at the end some articles of mine about business ethics, because I wanted to.

Daniel Greenberg

September 2017

ii

THANKS

Many thanks to Julia, Yisroel, Avi, Shira and Elisheva, and my parents, all of whom have been supportive of my bloggish efforts since their inception (and I'm sure Jenny and other Elisheva would have been had they known me at the time).

Many thanks also to Daniella Spector and Hannah Srour who worked hard getting this ready for publication.

It is also customary to thank God. I've never quite got my head around the notion of gratitude to God. For example, there is a notion in the laws of blessings that I should thank God for providing me with water when I'm thirsty; but since I wouldn't have been thirsty but for God I'm not quite sure that it makes sense. I've never been given a really convincing answer to the question why one should feel gratitude to God: but the closest anyone came was Dayan Lopian (see Chapter 32) who basically said we should feel grateful because it feels right when we are and wrong when we're not. And he was right: it does. So, thank you God.

iii

About the author

Daniel Greenberg is a lawyer specialising in legislation and the legislative process. He served in the Lord Chancellor's Department from 1988 to 1991 and in the Office of the Parliamentary Counsel (UK) from 1991 to 2010. From 2010 to 2016 he was an adviser in the Office of Speaker's Counsel, House of Commons and a consultant Parliamentary Counsel at Berwin Leighton Paisner LLP. In August 2016, he was appointed Counsel for Domestic Legislation in the House of Commons.

He also serves as the General Editor of Westlaw UK Annotated Statutes and Insight Encyclopaedia. He drafts primary and subordinate legislation in the UK, and has provided drafting and training services in Albania, Belfast, Cardiff, Edinburgh, Falkland Islands, Gibraltar, Isle of Man, Malaysia, Myanmar, Nigeria, South Georgia, Sri Lanka, the Solomon Islands and elsewhere.

He is also the Editor of Craies on Legislation, Stroud's Judicial Dictionary and Jowitt's Dictionary of English Law, the Editor in Chief of the Statute Law Review, the Editor of Halsbury's Laws on Statutes, and a contributing editor to the Oxford English Dictionary.

He is an Associate Fellow of the Institute of Advanced Legal Studies, University of London, a teaching faculty member of the legislative drafting course of Athabasca University, a Visiting Professor at the University of Derby, a Director of the Constitution Reform Group and a Fellow of the Bingham Institute for the Rule of Law.

Daniel has always had an interest in learning and teaching Jewish law and thought, and has been active in the Jewish community in that way for over thirty years. He wrote a series of articles for the Jewish Chronicle for a number of years, including a mini-series on Jewish business ethics which has always been a particular interest of his. He was involved in providing free tuition for prospective converts to Judaism for some years, particularly for those who could not afford a professional tutor; his thoughts on that process were encapsulated in his first book on Jewish matters – *How to Become Jewish and Why Not To* – which is still available in Kindle form from Amazon.

1

What if God's a Christian?

It is excellent to start off this book with a fake: it's a fake because although this is one of my favourite posts of all time, I issued it on the email circulation list that was the precursor to the Sceptic Blog, and I can no longer find a copy of the original text. So here it is, roughly in accordance with my memory of what I first said. The message remains clear in my mind, and so seminal that it had to form both the title and the first entry of this book.

Even the most hardened fanatic, who has trained himself or herself to listen to nothing but the promptings of bigotry and righteous indignation, must very occasionally wake in the small hours of the night and wonder what will happen if they turn out to be wholly or even partly wrong.

Of course, if religious people are so wrong that it turns out there is actually no kind of life whatsoever after death, then it probably doesn't matter very much what we do during our lives, for good or for bad.

But what if religious fanatics are right that there is a life after death, but wrong that it is presided over by a deity who sympathises with their particular form of bigotry? For me, it is this question that amounts to the inner promptings of a conscience and divinely created common sense – the kernel of the divine image in which all human beings are created – that is capable of grounding us in reality and recalibrating a mind that is tempted by attractive but implausible theological promptings.

Put simply, the world would be a much better place if every religious man and woman took for his or her guiding principle, not to do anything in the name of religion that he or she would have to come to be ashamed of after death if it became apparent that their particular religion, or their particular understanding of a religion, had been based on a false premise.

More importantly, the world might be able to enjoy institutionalised religion of all kinds as an overall force for more good than harm, which is the reverse of the present situation.

There is theological foundation for this approach within the earliest Jewish traditions. Our religion was discovered not by Moses the law-giver but by Abraham, who discovered and gave to the world two things, only one of which is commonly recognised and celebrated today. The Abrahamic religions are credited with having given the concept of monotheism to the world, and are by many moderate religious leaders believed to have unshakable bonds between them on that ground to this very day. And it is certainly true that Jewish tradition credits Abraham with having discovered the concept of a single God. According to rabbinic tradition, however, his more lasting legacy was the characteristic of *chessed* or kindness.

The connection between these two concepts is obvious: if there is a range of gods in the world then that naturally inspires competition and struggle for supremacy between the gods, or at least between their adherents.

If there is a single god of whom every human being is a creation, then there is no sense in human beings fighting each other since we are all effectively limbs of a single entity, and, on the contrary, we have as much reason to show kindness and concern to each other as brothers and sisters and other members of a single family.

For Abraham, it was this founding value of a benign God who creates everything that was much more important than the slightly technical question of how many gods there are. Abraham challenged God openly and defiantly as recorded in the Bible over questions of social injustice: the concept of collective punishment of the people of Sodom and Gomorrah troubled Abraham enough to turn to God and challenge him in words which amount to challenging God for appearing to betray his own fundamental principles of justice and fairness. Similarly, the troubling and extraordinary story of Isaac's near-sacrifice can be understood, if at all, in a similar vein, as I discuss later in this book.

Nobody can doubt that in the world today religion is, in its institutional forms, a source of more harm than good, and that its principal contemporary legacy to the world is violence and division.

I can easily understand how a person justifies to herself or himself performing the most appalling atrocities to other human beings in the name of a god, while they have managed to make themselves temporarily certain that that god really does exist and really does demand these apparently unpleasant things of them. But, to put it at its bluntest, it is a sound insurance policy for each person to reflect from time to time that his or her understanding of the divine will may, in the end, turn out to be inaccurate.

Belief as a concept is simply the absence of knowledge and the substitution of guesswork, based on tradition that may or may not have been accurately transmitted. For this reason alone, it makes sense for everybody to allow the promptings of conscience in the middle of the night to set the parameters of religious behaviour. Looked at simply in terms of insurance, if I do nothing in the name of religion that will cause me to be ashamed in later life or in after-life should happen to be one, then I cannot go far wrong. If I abandon that principle, I am unlikely to go far right.

PRAYER AND RITUAL

2

Praying for the Terminally Ill

Prayer is a common denominator of all religions (so far as I know). But it is also one of the baffling religious concepts. If God responds to prayers then why don't we all do it? But if God responds to prayers why is there so little evidence of it? And is prayer about asking for things anyway? Mostly it doesn't bother me and I pray by rote without worrying too much about what it's intended to achieve: but occasionally I can't prevent myself from wondering what exactly is going on – and I had a powerful and troubling instance of that when it suddenly dawned on me that we routinely pray for people who seem to be about to die, then they die, and then we all go to the funeral – and nobody either complains that the prayers didn't work or suggests that we stop bothering next time someone's ill: so what's the point? (From 28th December 2007)

I have only just realised something that should have been obvious to me all along (and probably is to others).

I have often felt uncomfortable wishing people *"refuoh shleimoh"* – complete recovery – on behalf of a relative or friend who is clearly terminally ill. Of course

I want to express sympathy with anyone who is ill or suffering: but is it apt to say *"refuoh shleimoh"* to the child of a ninety-nine year old parent who has clearly taken to their bed for the last time?

The answer is, yes – as I should have realised all the time – and it has nothing to do with miracle cures.

The prayer for the sick includes the passage *"refuas hanefesh u'refuas haguf"* – a cure for the soul and a cure for the body. And that is the point. Everyone needs both, all the time. If someone is on their way out of this world, I am praying that they should leave with their soul at rest. And it is never too late to pray for that.

3

Praying for Peace

With the increasingly prevalent trend towards the de-legitimisation and demonisation of Israel as a Jewish state, it becomes even more important than it always was for Jews around the world who love the state and every-thing it stands for to show that love in a careful and dis-criminating way, that acknowledges faults and is careful to applaud only when and where applause is deserved and appropriate. For those of us who are careful to avoid jingoistic and undiscriminating endorsement of actions of the Israeli government while remaining strong supporters, it is always disappointing (although perhaps not surprising) when the media fails to appreciate the subtlety of the distinction. (From 11th January 2009)

The BBC report of today's rally in Trafalgar Square reports that there was "a festival atmosphere as people cheered and applauded a succession of speakers who called for peace for Israel and the Palestinians".

Oddly enough, this is one piece of inaccurate report-ing that really upsets me.

I was in Trafalgar Square, and saw nothing like a fes-tival. There was certainly applause, as speakers called for peace for innocent people everywhere. But the applause, like the speeches themselves, was noticeably muted and restrained.

This was no victory rally – nor was there any hint of exhorting Israel towards a military victory. It was clear from the banners, the speeches and from the behaviour and sombre reactions of the crowd that nobody saw this as a war to be measured in military terms, but only as a necessary and unlovely precursor to peace for everyone. There was no suggestion that the side with the fewest casualties or fatalities will have "won" – only sadness that so many innocent people should have to suffer before a secure peace can be declared. When we arrived, there was a song of peace being played over the Tannoy: as we dispersed, the crowd sang a song that puts a prayer for peace to music.

In yesterday's parashah, Yaakov asks not to be buried in Ancient Egypt, but to be "lifted up" and carried back to be with his fathers in the Cave of the Patriarchs. And he insists, apparently unnecessarily, on Yosef making a formal oath to that effect.

The oath was not for Yaakov's sake, but for his descendants. We are bound by that oath forever to perpetuate the memory of our father Yaakov by lifting it up, by our behaviour, above the cruelty and selfishness that he associated with the culture that prevailed in the land where he died and where we were later enslaved.

The Jewish people are bound by that oath to regulate our standards of behaviour in all matters – personal, institutional and national – not against the behaviour of others, past or present, but against the high standards that our fathers Avrohom, Yitzchok and Yaakov demanded of themselves and of us.

I know nothing about Israeli politics or military strategy. But I know that Israel proclaims itself a Jewish state, and that I can be ashamed when it fails to live up to Jewish standards, and proud when it tries to do so.

When Israel makes a humanitarian-aid corridor because it argues that it is the proper thing to do, I can be proud.

And when Jews stand in Trafalgar Square when Israel is at war – a war which in purely military terms it could be said both to be winning and always to have been bound to win – and do not rejoice at or pray for victory, but pray only for peace for all, we can all be proud and we can all be hopeful.

4

Praying together

This piece represents my first thoughts on seeing variant behaviour within a particular synagogue. I should add, however, that those who habitually pray in that synagogue take a much more generous spirited view the night of the variation, and regard it as symptomatic of a healthy diversity of religious approaches. And since they live there, so to speak, and I merely visit occasionally, their view is infinitely more authoritative than mine, as well as being far more wholesome and less cynical. (From 28th December 2007)

Having just returned from Israel, I have to report that what I thought might be a short-lived nonsense is gathering momentum. On entering a shul too often you find most of the congregants praying towards the Aron HaKodesh, but a small number insisting on facing somewhere towards the corner, having calculated precisely the direction of Jerusalem.

This kind of holier-than-thou and holier-than-our-fathers attitude undermines the entire purpose of davening as a kehillo – unity. Instead of presenting a united front, gaining from each other's strengths and compensating for each other's weaknesses, we present ourselves like this to God as a divisive and divided rabble.

In each shul, the rabbi should decide in which direction to daven (almost certainly simply towards the Aron): and then everyone should do so. Anyone who feels too holy for the congregation, should go elsewhere.

5

Carlebach Minyanim and Nigunim

In the Sceptic Blog, I have tried to challenge people to think about a number of things that have come to be taken for granted. The phenomenon of the "Carlebach minyan" – a singing-based form of prayer service named after one of its principal exponents of the 20th Century – has become more popular and widespread after his death than it was when he was alive. But there are some people who consider the phenomenon more than a little insensitive, in the light of accusations against Shlomo Carlebach of a range if inappropriate behaviours. The opposite of love is famously identified not as hate but as indifference: communal indifference as to whether or not people suffered as victims and, if so, how they were treated, is an inexcusably complacent basis for elevating someone into iconic status as an emblem of prayer and introspection. (From 27th December 2016)

This has been worrying me for a while.

Shlomo Carlebach wrote wonderful tunes that without doubt help people to make their prayer and song spiritually richer.

But some people say he also behaved inappropriately: there are allegations of sexual abuse of minors and of other sexually inappropriate behaviour.

These allegations are anecdotal and appear online in a few places: so far as I can discover, during his lifetime he was never charged formally with any offence.

There may be something in these allegations; and there may be nothing in them.

So – "innocent until proved guilty" and sing on?

I'm not sure it's so simple.

If I were a victim of sexual abuse by Carlebach, how would I feel every time I saw another Carlebach Minyan starting up? And how would I feel every time one of his songs was started up to turn a service into a rousing chorus?

I would feel neglected by a community that seemingly doesn't care whether or not I was abused.

Having thought about it for a while and investigated a little bit online, it seems to me that the allegations are sufficiently serious to need some kind of investigation (the only investigation I have seen mentioned online does not seem to me to have been sufficient). The international Jewish community should find a way of setting up a credible investigation into the allegations, followed by a report (difficult, but not impossible – there are some precedents we could draw on). That report would either conclude that it is beyond reasonable doubt that Carlebach behaved improperly; or that there is no credible evidence that he behaved improperly; or that there is some credible evidence, but insufficient to be sure either way.

After that, individuals could make up their own mind about what that meant for their own attitude to his music.

But until then, the only message we are giving is that we don't really care. To embroider a theme from *Blowing In The Wind*, if we have sufficient ears to hear the beauty of Carlebach's music, we should have an equal ability and desire to listen to the cries of those who claim to have been abused by him

6

Cutting Pieces from the Machzor

It appears to be natural for the orthodox Jewish community to patronise and look down on the non-orthodox as a matter of course. It seems to be assumed that they would be orthodox if they were only committed enough, or spiritual enough, or good enough ... And oddly enough a large part of the non-orthodox Jewish world seems only too happy to accept a condescending and patronising attitude from the orthodox community without complaint; perhaps in some cases it assuages an element of guilt by those who have a sneaking feeling that they ought to practice more than they do? In any event, it is very dangerous for a number of obvious reasons. That aside, it is simply wrong to assume that because a person is not punctilious in matters of orthodox Jewish observance, and because they may not be well-versed in the language of orthodox prayer, their prayers are less important and it can be assumed that anything liturgically complex is likely to be beyond their understanding or appreciation. If services are boring, it is unlikely to be the fault of the early rabbis who composed complex and beautiful liturgical poetry, but of the settings within which those poems are read or sung.

Cutting out bits of the liturgy because they are perceived to be "boring" for the non-observant will certainly lead to shorter services (or it would if the rabbi didn't take up the slack with stultifyingly long sermons) but it will not lead to more engaging or dynamic services. (From 18th September 2005)

As shuls all over the world prepare for the Yomim Noro'im[1], the perennial question is raised at board meetings and between honorary officers: should we shorten the services by leaving out parts of the machzor[2] that nobody finds important or inspiring?

Particular targets for omission are the piyutim – liturgical poems interpolated for yomim tovim between parts of the regular daily prayers – which are generally replete with obscure Biblical or midrashic allusions and written in poetic language which is hard for all but expert scholars to understand and appreciate.

Whether it was permitted to interpolate these poems was originally a halachic debate. See, in particular, Shulchan Oruch Orach Chayim Chapter 68 and compare the attitude of Rabbi Yosef Caro, who is inclined to discourage these additions, with that of Rav Moshe Isserles who notes that for the Ashkenazim at least they have become traditional.

The Chofetz Chayim discusses these different attitudes to the piyutim (Mishneh Brurah note 4) and concludes that the most important principle is not to depart from the established traditions of each shul. In the biography

---

[1]   Rosh Hashanah and Yom Kippur – the "Days of Awe".
[2]   Special prayer book for those days.

of the Chofetz Chayim by his son, however, we learn that the Chofetz Chayim himself did not try to say all the piyutim prescribed by the traditions of the shul in which he was praying, but would focus intently on the meaning of a smaller number.

There is no contradiction between what the Chofetz Chayim writes and what he practised. The former is the correct rule for the shaliach tzibbur or chazan and for the formal order of service in each shul: not to depart from the established local traditions. For each individual, however, it is impossible to concentrate intently upon every single prayer of the Yomim Noro'im, and what is important is to pray at a rate, and with a liturgical rhythm, adapted to each person's linguistic capabilities, spiritual needs and personal circumstances.

For a shul to formally omit a passage from the service is to assume a frightening responsibility of deciding what is important and inspiring for all congregants. But what inspires one person may leave his or her neighbour cold. And what inspires me today may not do so tomorrow.

Those who attend orthodox services do so because they wish to be part of a chain of liturgical history. A man or woman may attend shul only once or twice a year: but it would be an error to assume that he or she must therefore wish the service to be as short as possible, or "modernised" by the removal of obscure passages. It may be that what moves the occasional attender most about the shul experience is the feeling of timelessness, and the knowledge of participating in the same service as that enjoyed by his or her parents and grandparents. Who knows what parts of the liturgy will be most reminiscent for that person of his or her childhood visits to shul, and how can I take the responsibility of "removing" from the service an obscure passage that may catch the imagination and open the heart of someone who has never prayed properly before in his or her life?

For Ashkenazim, our yomim Noro'im prayers will start properly next weekend with the first slichos[3] service. Between then and the final strains of tefilas geshem[4] on shemini atzeres, the machzorim will place in front of each of us the annual range of ideas and emotions, hopes and fears, lessons and aspirations. May we each find the right selection and balance among the available prayers to fashion into the most appropriate dialogue with God to build a good foundation for the coming year.

---

[3] Penitential prayers.
[4] Prayer for rain – said on Shemini Atzeres – the first of the final two days of the festival period beginning with Sukkot.

7

Brit Milah – The Painful Truth

Circumcision is institutionalised ritual child abuse – or the continuation of a holy tradition many thousands of years old. It all depends on your perspective. How do you convince a completely non-religious person that circumcision should be permitted on religious grounds? You don't, probably. And the worst way to try is to engage in medical arguments that neither side is likely to win in a convincing way. Better to accept that this is one of our strangest traditions, that it has its troubling aspects, and hope that people will be tolerant of an ancient tradition even if in some significant ways it jars with modern values. (From 17ᵗʰ November 2005)

Brit milah is a surgical procedure. So it can be tempting to think that medical science will have advice to offer about it. But, then as now, the most frequent form of advice will be simply "don't do it"; and if the medical community are treated by us as having a special standing in relation to brit milah, they will not hesitate to take reasonable advantage of that to expound upon the physical or psychological harm that their scientific knowledge leads them to expect to result from it.

Parashas Vayeiro opens with Abraham recovering from his brit milah at a place belonging to a man called Mamrei who is not mentioned before or after this event. The rabbis want to know why Mamrei deserves this express and apparently unnecessary mention in the Torah. Rashi answers from Bereishis Rabboh that "Mamrei gave Avrohom advice about the brit milah and therefore Hashem revealed himself to Avrohom on Mamrei's property".

So what advice did Mamrei gave Avrohom that merited such a reward? The Midrash Tanchumo records that Avrohom had three friends whom he consulted about brit milah. The first friend warned him that it would weaken him to such an extent that he would be vulnerable to reprisals from allies of the kings whom he had recently conquered. The second warned him that the loss of blood would be fatal. The third, Mamrei, expressed surprise that Avrohom should ask for advice and suggested that someone who had already experienced miracles, including being saved from being thrown into a furnace, should have sufficient confidence in Divine protection simply to fulfil the direct command of Hashem.

So Mamrei's advice consisted in refusing to give advice!

Mamrei's message to Avrohom Ovinu was to disclaim on the part of the scientific community any right to advise about the methodology or effects of brit milah, any more than in relation to any of the other mitzvos which we have in direct command from Hashem.

I have occasionally heard arguments, on the radio or elsewhere, between rabbis and doctors about brit milah. The doctors have won every time. While the rabbis assert repeatedly that brit milah causes no significant pain and does no lasting harm, the doctors not only deny it but adduce evidence (as to the quality of which I am ignorant) of occasional physical harm; and they regularly assert the possibility of long-term trauma.

Brit milah is not something we would ever have invented for ourselves: it is counter-intuitive for us, not only as Jews commanded to love others but even simply as sensitive human beings. But the Ksav Sofer on Devorim 22:6 (discussing the connection made by Devorim Rabboh 6:1 between brit milah and kan tzipor) explains that the essence of performing brit milah is that a person should feel the apparent cruelty of harming his defenceless child, and should nevertheless perform the brit in recognition that human understanding of cruelty or kindness is imperfect, and fades into irrelevance when faced with a clear and direct Divine command.

So we conquer our instincts and perform brit milah with the same obedience (although not necessarily unquestioning obedience) to the tradition handed down from Abraham Ovinu to the present day as that which underpins our entire commitment to Torah.

Anyone who performs brit milah cheerfully and asserts that it causes no significant pain, not only misses this message but contradicts the ruling of the rabbis that at the seudas mitzvah for a brit milah we omit in birchas hamozon[5] the celebratory introduction that we include at a sheva brochos, on account of our consciousness of and sensitivity for the baby's suffering.

Much of what we do as Jews must seem extraordinary to others, and brit milah must seem not just

---

[5] Prayer after a formal meal.

extraordinary but barbaric. If we meet charges of barbaric cruelty with scientific argument or merely with unfounded protestations, we cannot expect other than the most hostile and contemptuous opposition. If we admit the apparent cruelty but present our commitment to this practice as based on devotion to, and trust in, a revealed Divine tradition transmitted to us throughout the generations, we can at least hope that our honesty will be regarded with an uncomprehending respect.

8

Tefilin – Ignorance and Arrogance

Much of what we do as Jews must appear as odd to the non-Jewish world as the brit milah, although mostly more harmless. Wearing boxes of leather containing biblical verses is, on the face of it, a distinctly odd thing to do judged by any objective standard. Like most of the rest of our ritual, it doesn't harm or interfere with anyone else and in a modern secular liberal county we can hope to be left to get on with it without interference. But just occasionally it requires to be carried on with just a smidgen of that rare but valuable commodity, common sense. (From 31st January 2010)

The boy who caused a security alert by wearing tefilin on an airplane clearly had no common sense. Worse than that, he was reflecting a prevalent communal attitude that for non-Jews not to know instinctively all about us is culpable ignorance on their part, an attitude which of course in reality merely reveals monstrous arrogance on our part.

I have always wondered why Rashi finds it necessary, when the word "totafot" is used in the Chumash to describe tefilin (Shemos 13:16), to quote a Talmudic opinion that it is a compound word formed from two foreign words including an African one. Why is this thought worth telling us? (One might even wonder why the Rabbis thought able to attribute a word of Loshon Hakodesh[6] to a compound of two pre-existing foreign words; something for another time.)

As the Rambam discusses in Moreh Nevuchim, many of our mitzvos have their counterpart in other religions, while some are exclusive to Judaism. And it is important to know which is which: apart from anything else, knowing whether one of our strange rituals is in fact sufficiently common to other religions to be likely to be recognised and understood by others can help to avoid misunderstandings, not to mention security alerts on airplanes. So perhaps Rashi wants us to know that this particular ritual had a rough equivalent in at least two other cultures of the time. Nowadays, of course, there is no equivalent of tefilin in any of the religions of which most of us have heard (although it would not surprise me to learn that there is an equivalent in some religion somewhere).

There is good Biblical precedent for the idea that we should go out of our way to ensure that our religious practices and ideas will be understood by others in their own terms. When Moshe Rabbeinu describes our history to the King of Edom (Bamidbar 20:15) he says that Hashem sent an angel to bring us out of Mitzrayim. We spend half of Seder night each year saying that Hashem took us out personally and not by angel – so

---

[6] The Biblical Hebrew language.

why does Moshe change the story? Again, perhaps because the King of Edom could reasonably be expected to understand and accept the notion of an angel intervening, that being within the sphere of his own religious ideas, but would not be able to understand the notion of a single, infinite God.

Common sense is always useful, and never common. It behoves us to remember that we are a tiny minority of the people of the world, and that we should have the humility to remember that if we want our strange practices to be tolerated and even appreciated we should be prepared to take a few moments to explain them in terms that other people can understand and accept.

9

The Jewish All-Blacks –
Double-Sided Tefillin Straps

This piece is another where a relatively trivial technical point of ritual observance made me think about a wider trend within orthodox Judaism. The explanation of the selection of Mount Sinai discussed in the third paragraph is a minor extension of a classic rabbinic teaching that the mountain was chosen as being the most "humble". As religious observance today, certainly within orthodox Judaism, seems to be a constant race towards the top of exclusivity and expense, in order to be able to reach heights from which one can look down on as many others as possible, perhaps this is one of the most important issues facing Jewish practice today; sufficiently important for it to be worth sacrificing innovations in ritual observance, even if they may be mild improvements, for the sake of preserving a community of which everyone can feel an equal and equally-valued part. (From 9th December 2007)

Before the new fashion for double-sided tefilin straps (black on both sides) takes hold, it is important to try to squash it, on a number of grounds.

First, these will certainly be more expensive than the single-sided straps. So this is just one more attempt to raise the stakes in the observance game, making it an increasing burden on those of limited income to feel that they are doing justice to their religious obligations and providing unnecessary extra opportunities for those who wish to play holier-than-thou games of one-upmanship.

The Torah was given on the smallest mountain – Mount Sinai – to teach a lesson: if we all set out to climb Everest, most of us will fail, and only one or two of the fittest will be able to dance around on the top looking down on the rest. But if we all set out to climb a small hill, we can all get there: some of us will need to help others, and we will proceed at different paces – but soon we will all be able to stand there together and draw on each other's strengths and weaknesses in worshipping God as a united whole community. So we should always be suspicious of anything that purports to set the standards of religious observance in a way designed to exclude – or likely to have the effect of excluding – being beyond the easy reach of everyone who wishes to be part of the Jewish community.

Secondly, since we have a principle of *yeridas hadoros* – that the further we get from Sinai the less our religious instincts are to be trusted – we should be suspicious of anything that implies that the religious observance of former generations was lacking. If a new technological development enables us to achieve standards not available to our fathers or grandfathers, we should welcome it as they would have. But our grandfathers had black ink – if they had wanted to colour both sides of the straps they would have done.

Thirdly, it is a halachic requirement that the straps be straight at all times when I am wearing my tefilin. At present, I can quickly see when they are crooked, because the raw leather shows: with two black sides, it will be more difficult to notice.

Devotion to *mitzvos* is the essence of our religion. Endlessly seeking to make religious life more difficult for ourselves and others is not. (Personal *chumros* – stringencies – that do not impinge upon others, directly or indirectly by making them feel inadequate, are a wholly different matter.)

10

Beyond the Fringe –
Techeiles Tzitzit

*This is another apparently rather technical piece, about
the colouring used for the fringes on Jewish ritual gar-
ments. But there is an underlying point of some general-
ity and importance, about hypocrisy. There may be
some valid religious reasons for using the new blue dye
on those fringes that are publicly visible, and not on
those which are hidden from view. But one suspects
that at least in some cases the motivation is simply
that it seems worthwhile to spend the extra money for
those parts that can be seen, while for those parts that
are hidden the beer minimum that can be spent to
satisfy the basic religious requirement is all that can be
justified. To that extent, this is a slightly disturbing
analogy for much wider aspects of religious behaviour.
(From 28th December 2007)*

The new-fangled fashion for blue-threaded tzitzit continues to attract new adherents, both here and in Israel.

There is no sign that the general feeling of the gedolei
Yisroel is moving towards acceptance that the blue dye

presently on sale is indeed the chilozon dye required for Techeiles.[7]

But there are certainly those who say that it is; and they are, of course, entitled to follow their opinion, or their rabbi's.

But one thing strikes me as clearly wrong. I see many people wearing Techeiles tzitzit on their tallis godol, but ordinary tzitzit on their tallis koton. Either the new dye is Techeiles or it is not. If I think it is, then I cannot perform the mitzvoh in any other way – so to wear a four-cornered garment (my tallis koton) without Techeiles is to transgress a Biblical prohibition. If it is not Techeiles, then to put it on the tzitzit of my tallis godol is to colour the tzitzit inappropriately (we use white not as an alternative colour but as the absence of colour, in default of Techeiles).

Let people either wear or not wear the new dye; but each person should be consistent.

---

[7] Skye blue colour originally used for fringes; but no longer used widely as there is no longer any generally accepted source (it used to come from a kind of mollusc, but most people are not sure which was used).

THE JEWISH YEAR

11

Shabbat UK –
A Grump's Eye View

Perhaps the most sceptical part of the Sceptic Blog is a suspicion of anything that everybody else seems to be satisfied with. There is an intriguing rule of Jewish law that if all 71 members of a Jewish criminal court (Sanhedrin) are satisfied of a defendant's innocence, then the defendant is acquitted – on the grounds that any group of 71 who are completely convinced of some-thing and see no points of doubt must have missed something, and must have become led away by some kind of group-think. So with the Chief Rabbi's annual Shabbat UK event – which aims to involve the whole of the community in some aspect of Shabbat – if everyone seems satisfied that it's a wholly good idea, there must be something wrong with it ...? *(25th October 2014)*

This week thousands of people in the UK, and hundreds of thousands world-wide, took part in what looks set to be an annual event to bring normally non-observant Jews closer to Shabbat observance and community participation.

What could possibly be wrong with that?

Nothing, except ... that it may possibly give some people a misleading view of what Shabbat observance is about.

The Talmud records that if every Jew keeps Shabbat twice consecutively, the Messiah will come.

Why require two Shabbatot? The organisers of this week's Shabbat UK will probably be able to testify to how difficult it is to engage lots of people to do it just once!

The point is, that Shabbat observance is not about the Shabbat day itself, it is about how our Shabbat influences the week that follows and is shaped by the week that precedes it.

To come together once a year to bake challos, try not to drive to shul, and invite guests to the Shabbat table, is all terrific stuff – excellent for the community, great for engagement, and simply a lovely experience: but it's not Shabbat.

Shabbat is a continuum: on Friday night it reflects a softening retreat from the harsh realities of the previous 6 days (hence the word "boh" in the feminine singular in the Friday night prayers); on Shabbat morning it reflects a strength of purpose to concentrate on a day of spiritual re-charging (hence the word "bo" – masculine singular); on Shabbat afternoon it reflects a preparation for the 6 days to follow and connection with the endless series of 7-day cycles that are the essence of Shabbat observance (hence the word "bam" – plural form – even in those nuschaot[8] which do not use the word "Shabbatot" at that point).

---

[8]   Liturgical versions.

Shabbat is not a novelty, or a single event of high spiritual excitement. Shabbat is a way of life, a participation in a cycle that repeats itself endlessly and sublimely, irrespective of whether we keep it fully, partly or not at all. "More than the Jews have kept Shabbat, the Shabbat has kept the Jews": this famous epigram is about Shabbat observance as an individual expression of a person's unshakeable relationship with God, and not about Shabbat as an opportunity for community growth.

So a lovely idea, and a lovely occasion: but let people who have tasted it remember that they have not yet tasted the real thing – that will come if they put their 'phones down and turn off the television and put away the car next week, and the week after, and the week after ... And as the Talmud says, once all Jews have observed a week with a Shabbat at each end, enriched by spiritual preparation and crowned by spiritual fulfilment, then the Messiah will come; or, rather, he will already be here.

12

Seder Night

An unusually straight-forward piece by me drawing attention to the key points of the Pesach Seder. (From 7th April 2006)

We sometimes tell the children that on Seder night we are celebrating being free. That is not quite true. In fact, we are commemorating three different things in three different ways: the fact that we were slaves, the process of becoming free and the fact that we became free. The maror commemorates our slavery. The matzoh commemorates the process of becoming free, leaving Mitzrayim too fast to stop to let the dough rise. And the mitzvoh of haseivoh – leaning – commemorates being free.

As we say at the start of the Seder (ho lachmoh anyo), although the slavery of mitzrayim is past, in each generation there are other things to which we become enslaved. Sometimes it is a physical slavery forced on us, as Pharaoh did. Sometimes it is a seductive culture to which we enslave ourselves, with even greater spiritual danger than the physical slavery (tze ul'mad – Pharaoh only threatened the males while Lovon threatened everybody). We need to work out each year whether we are facing a Pharaoh-kind of slavery or a Lovon-kind of slavery: coercion from without or temptation from within. As HaRav Lord Jakobovitz z'tzl used to put it, some generations have to learn to survive adversity, our generation's principal challenge is to learn to survive relative prosperity.

Of these three mitzvos of the Seder, the one which we perform most closely to the mitzvoh as performed in Pesach Mitzrayim, the mitzvoh which everybody agrees is mid'oraisoh bizman hazeh – Biblically required even when we do not have the Temple – is matzoh, which commemorates the process of becoming free. It commemorates the fact that while we could have strolled leisurely away from Egypt, confident in God's protection from our enemies, we rushed out without time for the dough to rise, desperate to leave behind a culture of greed and materialism and to put ourselves in a simplistic and trusting way (chessed n'urayich) under the protection of God in an environment of material difficulty but spiritual purity. That is the essence of the Seder, reminding ourselves that what the Jewish people have achieved once we can achieve again, and that we can free ourselves from all those influences and habits which are contrary to Torah values.

And all the time that we are making that commemoration, we have the message of the four/five cups confronting us on the table. The Talmud records a dispute over whether we should drink four or five cups. The long-accepted custom is to drink four but to acknowledge the other opinion by having a fifth cup, Elijah's, on the table. Why not ordain five cups, on the grounds that by drinking five cups we would certainly satisfy both opinions? Because the cups commemorate the expressions of redemption used in the Torah: the fifth expression, "and I will bring you in" is a promise yet to be fulfilled, with the establishment of the third Temple. When we have completed the process of becoming free from today's slavery, and the third Temple is up and functioning, then we will be able to drink the fifth cup of redemption together and look back upon all kinds of spiritual and physical slavery as things of the past.

I wish everyone a happy and liberating yom tov.

13

Chad Gadya – A Spiritual Cycle

Some years ago, I decided that as a general rule I would not write down any Torah thoughts that I taught based on my own ideas, on the principle that if the thought was a really good one I would probably remember it and if I didn't remember it then it probably wasn't worth repeating. I still more or less stick to this rule, and have followed it in the Sceptic Blog by only writing down thoughts that I have already remembered often enough to teach more than once. The psychological explanation is one of my favourites, both because it hopefully adds relevance to what is generally a rousing but puzzling end to the Passover Seder, and because it draws on some key rabbinic ideas and puts them together in what I hope is an intriguing way. (From 31ˢᵗ March 2015)

Every year at the Seder table we all notice that the "wise" and "wicked" sons use similar terminology in talking about the Pesach, but only the wicked son is rebuked. They both say something along the lines of "what does this mean to you", without including themselves. Lots of explanations are offered, and the one that strikes the strongest chord with me sees the four sons as four generations.

The "wise" son is "clever" in a pejorative sense – a common use of the Hebrew "chochom" – he thinks he will make Judaism easy for himself by saying to his father – "tell me what the rules are but don't bother me with the explanations – I'll do whatever you do because I want to be 'frum' and stay within the exclusive social circle, but I don't see the need to search for complicated explanations; just tell me what to do and I'll do it".

The problem is that his son is the "wicked" son in the sense of liking to challenge things: he says to his father – anything you can explain to me so that I can understand it, I'll do – but anything that makes no sense to me, I won't. For example, why can't I use a light switch on Shabbos? But his father can't answer that, because he never asked his father, because he never wanted to understand. Social conformity was the extent of his religious observance. So the "wicked" son rejects everything that does not have an obvious explanation, and practices those parts of the religion that happen to make sense to him.

So his son is "simple" – the word "*tam*" in Hebrew meaning closed or deficient: he has a limited menu to choose from because he is starting from the list that happened to make sense to his father, who rejected everything he couldn't understand and whose father couldn't explain the others because he never asked about them.

Which means that the next generation "cannot ask a question" – he cannot put together a coherent question to establish the nature and value of his Jewish identity, because all he has is a few cultural fragments that happened to survive the ravages of both the "wicked" and the "simple" generations.

From complete Jewish observance to nothing at all in four generations: and all starting with blind, meaningless observance. So we warn the "wise" son: but in what terms? He is about to make a fundamental error in Jewish observance, so we say to him something profound and meaningful, presumably? Apparently not. We say: "don't eat after the Afikomen", the final piece of matzah at the Seder. Not obviously either deep, instructive or even relevant!

The Afikomen of the Haggadah is the Chad Gadya poem. Whatever differences there are in different Haggadot – and one of the key Seder rituals is comparing different orders and phrasings – every Haggadah around the world ends with Chad Gadya. This is the Afikomen that the Rabbis wanted to leave running around our minds at the end of the evening. And on its surface it is a children's tale about animals and other things without any profound message at all.

The central feature of the Chad Gadya is the small goat that father brings home for the Seder. This obviously represents the korban Pesach – the Pascal sacrifice.

The most superficial and selfish part of my mind looks on that simply as a good meal. The feline part of my nature – and cats are a byword for selfishness, and were one of the Egyptians' gods for that reason – wants to look no further into the korban Pesach than a nice meal. So the cat eats the goat.

But there is part of my nature that can't help thinking that we can do better than that as a religion, and that we need to look for something more meaningful. The canine part of my nature is looking for an ideal to sign up to and be loyal to. The dog has always been noted for loyalty, but without discrimination: like Bill Sykes' famous dog, the dog will be loyal to whoever feeds it, whether he be saint or sinner. So the dog chases the cat away, looking for something better than mere selfish greed in my religious observance.

That's a positive sign, but easily corrupted. The blind loyalty of the dog is open to being seduced by every kind of foolishness that religious mis-observance has to offer. The Jewish people at their least discriminating become easy prey for the latest meaningless chumras and frumkeits (stringencies and religiosities) and quickly become a parody of religion rather than a genuinely religious community. And generation after generation we reduce ourselves to spiritual bankruptcy through an excess of empty piety, and God is forced to step in and "punish" us, to bring us back to a desire to see through the superficial trappings of ritual and to reach for a genuine spiritual message in our religion. As the parent disciplines the child out of true compassion and care, the stick comes and beats the dog.

When human nature began its journey with good intention, however far it has been corrupted since, it responds positively to adversity. The stick arouses a spark in the dog of contrition and submissiveness, looking for a master who is worth following; looking for kindness and sensitivity that can be reciprocated. The Jewish people come back to God with their figurative tail between their legs, looking for something beyond the self-congratulatory complacencies of their earlier frumkeits. The stick has reignited the spark of real spiritual yearning in the Jewish soul – the eternal flame of Torah comes and replaces the stick, making it unnecessary and irrelevant.

That yearning makes me receptive to true Torah learning, which has been symbolised by water in

Aggadic literature throughout the ages. The water of Torah – the purest liquid, sustainer of life, that always seeks the humblest and lowest place to occupy – quenches the spark of yearning and satisfies our thirst in a meaningful and constructive way.

The animal that drinks the pure water of Torah becomes loyal to God in a fully discriminating way: it has the strength and determination that is not distracted by superficial fancies because it has a deep knowledge and understanding of its true master. "The ox knows its owner", as we recite from the prophet around Tisha B'Av every year – and our soul that has been through the journey from selfishness, through corruption, to contrition and learning, knows God in a clear and truly spiritual way.

But along comes that most destructive of animals: man. The "slaughterer" destroys other peoples' spiritual ambitions and achievements for the sake of trying to make himself feel better about his own spiritual poverty. With a snub, an unkind word, or by making clever fun of someone else, we destroy their feeling of achievement and self-worth and send them back to the beginning. The same power of speech that created the world, is capable of destroying it in each of us when it is used destructively as it so often is.

The slaughterer feels a little better when he has proved to himself his superiority over the ox-like simpleton whose religious attainments were so easy to deride. He congratulates himself on his "cleverness" – the chochom who knows better than everybody else. But he and his victim both fall prey just as easily to the Angel of Death, who levels all, and sends them back to their Maker who restarts the whole cycle at His will.

And is that cycle doomed to continue without end? Will there never be a more permanent resting-place for those who seek spiritual comfort? Will there never be a "Next Year in Jerusalem" – an eternal atmosphere of peace and goodwill for the whole of humanity, living side by side in recognition of a single divine presence?

Of course there will. And it will begin when we break the vicious cycle ourselves, by supporting each other's spiritual ambitions and helping each other to achieve what we cannot do alone: building on each other's strengths, supplying each other's deficiencies and strengthening each other's weaknesses.

When the clever part of my mind – the "wise" son at the Seder table – is not satisfied with simply copying the outward rituals but wants to make sure that every religious observance is properly founded in understanding of a symbolism that enhances human sensitivity and encodes spirituality into human activity; when that happens, I start out on a religious journey that can join with yours to bring a Next Year in Jerusalem for the whole world.

So we warn the Chochom: don't eat after the Afikomen. Make sure the ritual of the Seder table lingers in your mind when you leave it and changes who you are. If you walk away from the Seder table the same person who sat down – you may as well not have bothered to come. But if you walk away having released yourself from Egypt – having identified a particular constraint of the material world and released yourself from it – and the lingering taste of the Afikomen changes your behaviour on the way home, in your house, in the street, shop and office the next day, then we are starting a journey that is really necessary.

14

Kitniot – Let The Buyer Beware

This piece is perhaps unusually technical for me. But it troubled me that kosher shops were unwittingly allowing people to buy products that were not appropriate for their own religious observances. Having brought this to the attention of a number of shop owners, I have the satisfaction that they now mislead consumers wittingly. (From 26th March 2008)

From what I see in the shops before Pesach these days, I fear that many people are unwittingly eating food on Pesach that is not kosher l'Pesach according to their own family and community traditions.

Kitniot – rice, beans and pulses – are not chametz. But the centuries-old ashkenazi minhag is not to eat them on Pesach, for any one of a number of possible reasons. The sephardi minhag has always been to allow kitniot on Pesach, and for them they are fully kosher l'Pesach.

An increasing number of foods manufactured for Pesach in Israel contain kitniot, to accommodate the sephardi majority. Even surprising things – ice-cream, mayonnaise, ketchup – routinely contain kitniot nowadays. But the fact is mentioned on the label only in very small Hebrew letters that can be difficult to find and decipher even for those who know what they are looking for.

The shops in London clearly have a duty to put up large notices warning the majority ashkenazi population in this country to watch out for kitniot; and they would do well to label each product on the shelves as kitniot-free or containing kitniot. I encourage everyone to bring gentle, polite and friendly pressure on the shopkeepers to do this for us.

Until they do, I am worried that many people who want to keep Pesach properly but are not well-versed in these issues and may not be able to read Hebrew are likely unwittingly to bring into their houses for Pesach use products which they would not want to use if they knew the full story.

15

Zimbabwe, Rwanda
and Mount Sinai

Back to the dangers of institutionalised religion ...
(From 7ᵗʰ June 2008)

On Shavuos we tell the children that Mount Sinai was chosen as the place for giving the Torah to the Jewish people because, being the lowest of the surrounding mountains, it represents humility, an attribute required for receipt of the Torah.

But there is another aspect to this symbolism. If we all set out to climb Mount Everest, we will all reach different points before giving up: only a very few will reach the summit, from which they will look down on the rest of us with the self-satisfaction born of having achieved what the rest of us could not. But if we all set out to climb a small hill, we can all make it to the top: of course, some of us will have to give others a helping hand, but one way or another we can all make it and reach the summit together.

Torah is intended to be a lifestyle that is realistically attainable by everyone. If it becomes a set of standards that are so demanding – whether financially or in terms of time or other commitments – that in practice only a very few can meet them, we know that we have gone wrong. Judaism is not about setting high and exclusive targets so that I can look down on all those who fail to meet them: it is about travelling together, on a spiritual journey from which nobody need feel excluded.

When I hear about terrible and inhuman things happening around the world, such as the recent genocidal violence in Rwanda or the present intimidatory violence in Zimbabwe, I worry about the numbers of people involved in making it happen. There will always be resho'im – wicked people – and for obvious reasons many of them will choose to wield political power. But if ordinary people were imbued with ordinary standards of human decency, the few resho'im would lack tools to carry out their wicked plans. It is the moral and ethical vacuum inside thousands of ordinary people that enables them to be corrupted into tools of other people's wickedness.

It should be literally impossible for one person to beat another with sticks until he is bleeding on the ground. It should be literally impossible for a group of soldiers to be incited to rape a group of women in a village. Our education and cultures around the world-wide should make it simply beyond the range of activity that an ordinary human being will permit himself or herself to undertake.

To have enclaves of people leading conspicuously holy lives is not a reflection of the Torah as given on Mount Sinai, a mountain representing universal attainment of basic spiritual goals. If religion is failing to set basic standards of universal morality that protect each of us from our worst sides and from corruption by the relatively few actively wicked minds, then religion is failing to achieve the task for which the world and it were created.

16

Barack Obama and Tisha B'Av

Another piece indulging my increasing monomania about the lack of synergy between religious practice and common sense. (From 3rd August 2008)

History repeats itself. The Temple was destroyed because as a nation we were abusing our privileged closeness to God, turning the sacrificial system into an excuse for arrogance, corruption and squabbling. The Temple was meant to be a source of spiritual light for the whole world ("my House shall be called a house of prayer for all the nations") and it became a source of shame, highlighting the spiritual bankruptcy of the generation.

This year, shortly before we come to the annual mourning for the destruction of the Temple, a non-Jew came to the last remaining wall of the holy edifice. Like millions of others from around the world, he wanted to take advantage of the closeness to God that everybody feels at this holy site, to put something of his heart onto paper and offer it to God.

So far, so good. Only some grubby-minded person, who portrays himself and possibly thinks of himself as an orthodox Jew, stole these private thoughts and sent them to a grubby-minded newspaper which published them, simply because the non-Jew is a candidate for the presidency of the United States of America.

As we sit on the floor this Tisha B'Av we can deepen our gloom by the knowledge that the present generation shows no less propensity than the generation of the destruction to abuse the Temple site for our own mean-minded petty purposes.

Until the generation whole-heartedly and publicly condemns this disgraceful act of indecency – until the thief is exposed and either publicly apologises and renounces his behaviour or is excommunicated – we can be sure that we do not deserve to rebuild the special bond between us and God that the Temple represented.

17

I'm Dreaming of a
Green Chanukah

*Orthodox Jews are not particularly known for their
environmental concern, which is surprising when one
thinks about the theoretical importance in Judaism
of cherishing God's creations and moving towards a
perfect world in partnership with God. I fear it's just
another instance of our spirituality being an excuse for
selfishness ... (From 8th December 2007)*

Certain environmentalists want us to curtail our Chanukah
observances to reduce carbon dioxide emissions. They
have calculated an impressive environmental impact to be
achieved by reducing our lighting by one candle each.

Much of secular conservation theory is at variance
with Jewish thought. In particular, the idea that human
beings should restrict themselves to sustainable uses of
the planet's resources, so that we do nothing that would
prevent the world from existing indefinitely, ignores the
Jewish belief that the world is not intended to last for
ever. The Talmud sees the world as intended as a relatively short-term project intended to last no more than a

few millennia – different precise lengths according to different rabbinic opinions.

But we share with environmentalists the idea that while the world exists we should use it sensibly. In particular, we have a number of environmental laws, such as, for example, town planning restrictions designed to prevent one interest group from polluting the environment for another.

To reduce our Chanukah lighting by one candle per night would make no sense halachically. But it might make halachic sense to go much further than that. While there are different opinions about the optimal number of lights to be lit, everyone agrees that just one light per person per night would satisfy the basic halachic requirement. The Jewish world has opted to exceed this, as a *hiddur mitzvah* – a beautification of the mitzvah. But it is no beautification to upset others or to add to their ecological difficulties.

It may be that the chemical global effect of the Jewish community resolving to return to the basic requirement of one light per person per night would be minimal, or even nugatory, as a reduction of emissions. But the spiritual effect could be explosive. It could demonstrate a real concern for our fellow human beings, and a real desire to do whatever we can to show sensitivity and a desire to avoid causing offence or discomfort. As a practical exercise in loving our fellow human beings and showing respect for their concerns and desires, it could kindle an eternal spiritual light of which we could be truly proud.

LAW AND ORDER

18

Copyright and Copywrong

It bothers me how little attention is given to the rules of day-to-day business ethics by orthodox Jews in general and Orthodox rabbis in particular. It is a great shame – and an uncomfortably revealing one – that the first major communal charity in London to fold as a result of the economic recession in the 1990s was the Jewish Association for business ethics. The Talmud records that the first question each person will be asked after death is whether he or she dealt honestly in their daily business activities. How troubling it is that many people will be unable to give a convincing answer to this question, simply because they have not considered sufficiently how different aspects of Jewish law applied to simple daily commercial transactions. How could, for example, handing out a sheet of sources for a Talmudic lecture Raise questions of Jewish business ethics... (From 3rd January 2017)

I sat in a shiur[9] a few weeks ago given by a rising star presently learning for a dayonus semichah (ordination

---

[9] Lecture.

as a judge of Jewish civil law) in a prestigious institution in America.

The handout included a diagram which he mentioned he had copied from a particular contemporary edition of a standard Jewish work.

After the shiur, I suggested that he should add to the handout the details of the permission given by the copyright owner for the reproduction, in order to avoid the prohibition of ma'aris ho'ayin (creating reasonable suspicion that he might have behaved improperly). He beamingly replied that this was why he had mentioned that he had copied the diagram, because that made it okay.

I had to explain that telling people where you've copied from doesn't make the copying lawful: any more than it becomes lawful for me to steal money from your pocket just because I tell the shopkeeper where I pinched it from when I spend it.

He thanked me politely, but I'm not sure he was convinced.

And he is going to be a dayan ...

(Even if they hadn't got around on the course to learning about intellectual property, you would hope that they would enter the course with enough common sense to work out for themselves that just saying where you got something doesn't make it yours.)

It's about time that everyone got the message that any shiur handout sheet that contains a reproduction from any work that is likely to be under copyright protection anywhere in the world should be treated like poison and avoided unless it clearly states that permission was sought and obtained, and recites compliance with any conditions.

(Anyone who thinks that so long as it's only a few pages nobody will care is wrong: a few years ago, Rabbi Cooper ztz'l asked me to make a few copies of the Terumah and Ma'ser Brochos from the Artscroll Siddur – I contacted Artscroll and although I only wanted to make a few copies for non-commercial use they were rightly careful to inquire into the precise circumstances, and they kindly gave their permission on specified conditions.)

Tzion b'mishpot tipodeh – which roughly translates as "Until we bring up our youngsters with a reasonably instinctive understanding of right and wrong, and an appreciation of the difference between *meum* and *tuum*[10], we might as well save ourselves the trouble of praying beseechingly and endearingly for Moschiach to come."

---

[10] Latin for mine and yours.

19

Chaim Halpern

The allegations of sexual impropriety against Rabbi Chaim Halpern caused enormous trouble at the time in the London Orthodox Jewish community. For a number of weeks there was a great deal of concern over the allegations and how they were being handled. There was much talk of ad hoc investigations by rabbis and dayonim; and much talk about whether there would be a police investigation and if so to what extent the orthodox community would cooperate with it. There was discussion in the Jewish newspapers (with the exception of those for whom news means only additional confirmation that everything in the orthodox world is fine, and the most exciting event is yet another successful visit by a foreign rebbe) and there was an unusual amount of discussion on the internet in various forums, much of it quite agitated. Within months, however, the whole thing had died down and was seen by everybody as a storm in a teacup; and the London Orthodox community has reverted to its self-congratulatory complacency. That is the real disgrace. If the allegations were true, we failed not only those victims but also every victim of abuse in the Orthodox community who will *now have had it confirmed that they may as well keep quiet and cry themselves to sleep because nothing except incompetence and muddle is to be expected of the handling of any public complaint that they might make. If the allegations were untrue, then others against whom untrue allegations may be made in the future will be able to comfort themselves with the same knowledge, that those allegations will be handled in such an inept fashion that any name that has significantly been sullied cannot fully be cleared. Since the prophets tell us in many places that redemption comes through the establishment of justice for the oppressed and disadvantaged, it is clear that our present stupefyingly complacent attitude to abuse and injustice within the community is a reliable recipe for delaying redemption – whatever that means – indefinitely. (From 30th November 2012)*

One way or another, a crashing injustice has been done and the London Jewish orthodox community should feel utterly ashamed of itself.

If Chaim Halpern did not abuse his position as a counsellor, then the community has allowed an innocent man to be hounded from positions of respect as a result of malicious gossip.

If he did abuse his position as a counsellor, then the community has sent a loud message to his victims that the closest they can expect to get to anything like justice is a messy cover-up.

If I were a girl or woman in the community today who was experiencing abuse from a communal leader, I would look at what has happened here and despair. I would not contact the police, because I would be afraid to; and I would not contact the rabbis, because the most

I could expect would be a kangaroo court in one of their houses resulting in some kind of messy compromise.

Mi k'amcho Yisroel – Who is like your people Israel? How often (do) we hear our leaders trumpet this phrase as they congratulate the community on its warmth and our kindness to each other.

That is absolutely worthless if there are victims in our community who are being allowed to cry themselves to sleep at night because nobody cares enough to stand up for them.

If Chaim Halpern abused women – whether or not he committed assault or any other crime – he should be publicly stripped of the title Rabbi and he should be placed in cheirem – excommunication – by every single rabbi in the area.

If Chaim Halpern did not abuse women – then every single Rabbi in the area should sign a paper stating that if anyone has evidence that he did they are not just permitted, but obliged, to take it to the police, and that unless and until a charge is brought the Rabbi is publicly upheld as a righteous and innocent person.

That neither of these things have happened, but a messy "deal" has been done behind closed doors, is such a disgrace that we cannot take ourselves seriously as a religious community until it is put right.

The Rabbis need to make one thing absolutely clear. If a person is abused by anyone in the community, whether or not they are sure that a crime has been committed, they are under a halachic duty to go to the police, and the Rabbis will give every encouragement and support to people who come forward in these circumstances. No closed-sessions of rabbis in each other's houses; no appointments of local lawyers to take down evidence and have it looked at by ad hoc Batei Din. Just a simple commitment to use the competent authorities of the State for those matters in which they are competent and the Beis Din is not (using the word competent in its legal sense).

This must not be allowed to blow over. Each one of us who belongs to the orthodox Jewish community in London will be confronted on the day of judgment and asked: Why did you, the Jewish public, allow this to go on in your name?

Irrespective of who is the victim.

20

Moiser and Planning Permission – An Ugly Myth

Having lived in so many countries without an effective rule of law, and having so often been the victims of the absence of any kind of community control, one might have thought that Jews would be attracted and committed to the rule of law in all its aspects. And, indeed, we do seem remarkably committed to it when it works in our favour; but sometimes our commitment to lawfulness appears to weaken a little when it looks as though it might become inconvenient. In particular, should it interfere with our wish to add never-ending tears of loft conversions to accommodate our burgeoning families, it is no longer merely inconvenient but has become practically heretical. What better way to avoid abiding by the same rules as our non-Jewish neighbours down to invent a biblical scruple that prevents us from cooperating with local authority planning regulations? Incidentally, when I consulted the late Dayan Lopian about this matter (for my assessment of him see Chapter 31) he thought for his customary few seconds and responded simply "Where are the Cossacks? Show me the Cossacks?"; and in this characteristically brief and whimsical way, he encapsulated in two short sentences everything that I seek to say below. (From 6ᵗʰ June 2010)

It seems to be being suggested with increasing frequency that Jewish people confronted with planning permission issues in relation to property owned by other Jews are not allowed to follow the planning permission procedures, but must arbitrate through a Beis Din.

This is nonsense (and, in so far as it is propounded by the Botei Din, distastefully self-serving nonsense).

The law of moiser ("informing") has two aspects.

First, there is a Biblical requirement to litigate in the Jewish courts and not in the civil courts (technically, nothing to do with moiser, but often wrapped up in assertions of its application). That is a firm prohibition of Jewish law. It gives way only where the Jewish courts are not competent to deal with the matter. So in the diaspora, anything criminal or with a criminal aspect goes straight to the secular authorities and courts; while even a financial dispute will be sent to the secular courts by the Beis Din if a party refuses to accept Beis Din jurisdiction or to comply with their orders.

Secondly, there is the prohibition against handing Jews or their property over to wicked Romans or Cossacks – or the contemporary equivalent from time to time – for unjust treatment.

There is, however, another little matter that is sometimes conveniently forgotten – dino d'malchuso dino. Jews are obliged by Jewish law to obey the law of the land: and in so far as this cannot be enforced by the religious courts it can be enforced through the secular courts.

With this background in mind, planning permission can be analysed as follows.

It is the law of the UK that I may not build certain structures without the local authority's planning permission. If I do, I have broken UK law and Jewish law. That is not a matter on which the Beis Din is competent in UK law: the Beis Din can arbitrate under the Arbitration Act, but that is appropriate for disputes about inter-personal liability, not for enforcement of breaches of the law. Since the Botei Din are not competent to deal with the matter, it is halachically permissible to use the secular courts.

As for moiser, the planning authorities are not wicked Cossacks arbitrarily pinching people's property: they are a branch of law enforcement, enforcing the law that forms part of the social contract to comply with which Jewish residents are bound by UK and Jewish law.

So to tell the local authority about a breach of planning permission is not halachically problematic. Indeed, it is an obligation, because when so-called religious Jews flout the law of the land they create a chilul Hashem.[11]

Equally, the idea that I may not participate in the statutory planning permission process by registering objections when asked by the local authority what I think about a neighbour's plans is absurd.

Unhappily, this is another example of ways in which purportedly religious Jews are prepared to misuse and manipulate concepts of Jewish law to permit them to behave unlawfully and unethically and to line their own pockets at other people's expense.

---

[11]   Desecration of God's name.

21

The Death Penalty (1)

It is probably just as well that the Torah reading is recited in orthodox congregations in Hebrew, despite the fact that this is a language which few present understand with fluency in the United Kingdom. Put bluntly, many who sit in approving silence throughout the weekly reading would be appalled if they actually understood more than a fraction of what they were listening to. (There are plenty of translations available today, of course, but people generally and sensibly don't bother to read much of them.) The death penalty, in particular, is one topic that many orthodox Jews would find it difficult to square with their consciences, as shaped by exposure to a western liberal civilisation. Of course, in today's conditions and the absence of a Jewish state (modern Israel being, even according to religious Zionists, not a Jewish state in that sense) the issue of capital punishment in Jewish law is purely theoretical. But it is as well to confront and become comfortable with the theory of any religion which one espouses ... (From 21st February 2008)

The victims' families in a murder case that concluded today have called for the reintroduction of the death penalty.

Jewish law and thought supports the notion of a death penalty. The Torah prescribes death as a penalty for a number of wrongs, including murder. And the executive powers of a Jewish King include powers of taking life.

The executive imposition of a death penalty can be justified in Jewish law by the need to deter others from a particular course of action. Of course, modern research sheds considerable doubt on the deterrent effectiveness of a death penalty, and that research would have to be taken into account in any modern re-application of the Jewish criminal code following the rebuilding of the Temple and the re-establishment of the Sanhedrin.

The judicial death penalty as prescribed by the Torah is not, however, expressly linked to deterrence. Rather, it is part of the Jewish notion of *kapparah* – atonement – that a person needs a way to purge himself or herself of the spiritual damage self-inflicted by the commission of a wrong. In some cases, such as a wilful murder, giving up one's life in this world may be the only effective way of moving in spiritual purity to life in the next.

The possibility of a miscarriage of justice is one which worries Torah judges and scholars to such an extent that the Jewish applied criminal laws are a mass of complexity, designed to make the execution of an innocent person a practical impossibility. An uncorroborated confession is insufficient, for example, there being many cases in which an imbalanced person will confess to a crime he or she did not commit. Indeed, it could almost be said that the Jewish death penalty is "voluntary", in the sense that there are so many opportunities for a defendant to oppose technical obstacles – such as objecting that he or she was not given an intelligible warning of the possible punishment before the commission of the crime – that one cannot see that anyone would actually be killed without in effect co-operating in the process.

Clearly, that is the essential issue, to ensure that there is no possibility of miscarriage of justice: easier said than done – no kind of evidence is unimpeachable, whether it be fifty witnesses who may all have conspired together or a DNA sample that may have been deliberately or inadvertently contaminated.

But, of course, it is a mistake to think that we need worry less about miscarriages of justice so long as we do not have the death penalty: imprisoning a person is potentially completely ruining their lives – and indeed the spiritual damage may in some cases be worse than that caused by the death penalty: which is why prison is not an approved Torah punishment, although it can be used as a preventative technique.

22

The Death Penalty (2)

When discussing this issue with students in the United Kingdom, I often begin by asking them whether they consider capital punishment or imprisonment the more barbaric. The answer is always, predictably, capital punishment. Then I take them through some of the literature issued by the Howard League for Penal Reform about concerns relating to prison; we talk about the recidivism rates from UK prisons, and we discuss some of the psychological implications of life imprisonment. Then we look at the issue of psychopathic murderers who are unlikely ever to be thought safe to release into society again, and we think about what kind of a life they are likely to have in captivity. And then I ask them the original question again. The answer is normally the same, but I generally have the satisfaction of seeing that they are a touch more hesitant about giving it. (From 13th December 2005)

This morning the American State of California executed a murderer. This is a comparatively rare event in America, and in most Western countries the death penalty is no longer used at all.

Around the world 122 countries have either renounced the death penalty or allowed it to become de facto obsolete: and the list of countries abandoning the death penalty grows at an average of 3 each year. But in 74 countries and territories around the world the death penalty is used, with varying degrees of frequency: in 2004, around the world 3,797 people were executed and another 7,395 sentenced to death. 97% of the executions took place in China, Iran, Viet Nam and the United States of America. Most countries use either hanging, shooting, electrocution or lethal injection. But Saudi Arabia and Iraq use beheading and Afghanistan and Iran use stoning. (The figures in this paragraph were taken from the website of Amnesty International – I have not attempted to verify them.)

There is a distinct ambivalence in the Jewish approach to the death penalty. On the one hand, our religious and natural principles of kindness and humanity cause us to recoil in horror from the idea of deliberate and cold-blooded killing of a human being, however guilty. On the other hand, we cannot forget that the Torah prescribes the death penalty for certain crimes, and that while this is not administered at a time when there is no Sanhedrin in the Temple precincts (Rambam, Hilchos Sanhedrin 14:13), it remains as much a part of Torah thought as any other mitzvah which is in temporary abeyance during the absence of the Temple and its attendant institutions.

It is clear that the same ambivalence is not only encountered but encouraged during times when the Sanhedrin is in place and the death penalty administered in accordance with Torah law. The Rabbis describe the degree of reluctance with which the dayonim approach the application of the death penalty, and condemn as "bloodthirsty" the hypothetical court that passes the death sentence as often as once in each seven years (Rambam, Hilchos Sanhedrin 14:10) (the Talmud records other opinions varying this period). And the halochoh of the imposition and administration of the death penalty shows many details designed to ensure not only that it is reserved for cases in which there can be no doubt as to guilt (and it is a staggering fact, again according to Amnesty International, that since 1973, 122 prisoners have been released in the USA after evidence emerged of their innocence of the crimes for which they were sentenced to death) but also that it is administered in as humane a way as possible. In particular, the modern pharmaceutical methods of ensuring insensibility prior to the act of killing find their counterpart in the halochoh (Rambam, Hilchos Sanhedrin 13:2) and would, were the death penalty reintroduced today with the re-establishment of the Sanhedrin, be one aspect of the halochoh that certainly both could and would be developed to embrace modern technological improvements. And the halochoh requires that once the judicial process is entirely concluded beyond all reasonable chance of reopening, administration of the death penalty is not delayed even by a single day, so as not to prolong the convict's period of suffering waiting to die (Rambam, Hilchos Sanhedrin 12:4).

Incidentally, one of the most contentious aspects of the debate about whether one can ever be sufficiently sure of a person's guilt to justify his or her execution concerns the use of confessions. While some regard it as an essential prerequisite of certainty, those with knowledge and experience of the processes of criminal law even in civilised countries that do not routinely interrogate by torture, regard confessions as sufficiently unreliable, for a variety of reasons, to make it unthinkable to rely upon an uncorroborated confession. And this receives interesting Biblical support: in Yehoshuah (7:21) we find that Achan admits his guilt on a charge of plundering and goes on to mention the order in which the spoils were hidden; and the Torah records (7:22) that on investigation the order given was found to be correct – possibly the earliest recorded instance of what is now the modern practice of regarding a confession as inherently unreliable unless it contains details of a kind that could not reasonably be expected to be known to anyone other than the criminal.

It is not the purpose of this short message to debate the issue of capital punishment in detail or at any length. But I wish to offer one observation, based on this week's parashah Vayishlach. When Yaakov struggles with and captures the angel, there is a puzzling passage in which he refuses to release the angel "unless you bless me" (Bereishis 32:27). This can be understood in a number of ways: one involves approaching the entire episode as an internal struggle of Yaakov with the evil inclination inside him (the "ish" that is always "imo" – 32:26). The rabbis (see, in particular, Michtav M'Eliyahu volume 2, essay on Parashas Vayeitzei) explain that Avrohom became expert in diverting his evil inclination, Yitzchok went further and became expert in confronting and destroying it, but Yaakov went further still and became expert in the even more demanding enterprise of converting his evil inclination into a positive influence. Hence the idea that he would not release the angel – end the struggle – until it had ceased to be a curse or threat and had become a positive influence or blessing (a thought which occurred to me and which I record here with the express approval of Rabbi Dovid Cooper *shlit'o*).

It is this idea of reclamation rather than destruction which colours the whole Torah approach to the treatment of offenders. Our starting point is always to aim for spiritual rehabilitation of even the worst criminal. Sometimes, the matter is taken out of our hands – where the Torah prescribes the death penalty and we are obliged to apply it as unquestioningly as we perform any other Divine commandment. But the cases in which the circumstances and evidence are such as to require the application of the death penalty in accordance with halochoh will necessarily be very few and far between. In the normal instance, we are left with considerable discretion as to the treatment of an offender, and in such cases our aim will always be to improve and reclaim, rather than merely to punish and to protect society (both of which are also duties). (Hence the well-known story in the Gemoro (Brochos) where B'ruria reminds her husband to pray not for the downfall of sinners but for the downfall of sin – and the sinners' rehabilitation.)

With this in mind the following comments of the Governor of California in relation to this morning's execution are particularly interesting—

"After studying the evidence, searching the history, listening to the arguments and wrestling with the profound consequences, I could find no justification for granting clemency. Stanley Williams insists he is innocent, and that he will not and should not apologise or otherwise atone for the murders of the four victims in this case. Without apology and atonement for these senseless and brutal killings, there can be no redemption."

So the Governor appears to have been significantly influenced by his assessment that the murderer did not have a sufficient appreciation of and remorse for his crimes to provide a foundation for spiritual reformation. Without that remorse – which in Torah thought also is an essential ingredient of teshuvah (Rambam, Hilchos Teshuvoh 2:2 and 3) – it will be impossible for the criminal to begin the three-stage process of diverting, confronting and finally transforming his evil inclination, and society will be unable to assist him in that process and will be able to address only the necessary duties of protection and punishment.

23

Provocation in Crime

Not only is the modern trend of beatifying Biblical characters troubling because it tends both to derive from and to exacerbate lack of discriminating thought in religious practice, but it is also directly contrary to rabbinic traditions. Here is a piece in which I drew on a radical (and little mentioned) interpretation of Sarah as having been distinctly less than perfect, and I extrapolated to offer some thoughts about criminal responsibility. (From 26th November 2005)

This week's parashah opens with an account of Avrohom eulogising and crying for Soroh who has just died. The word "and to cry for her" is spelled with a small letter chaf.

The Baal Haturim offers a primary explanation that because Soroh had lived such a full and long life Avrohom's grief was less extreme than had she suffered a tragically early death. Then he adds a secondary and alternative explanation: when Soroh challenged God to judge between her and Avrohom in the matter of her desire to expel Hagar from their home (Bereishis 16:5) she in one sense called down a judgment upon herself, as a result of which she was responsible for her own death – and we do not eulogise a person who is responsible for his or her own death. The first of these explanations makes immediate sense. The second is bewildering: how do we know that Soroh's death was connected with her demand for Divine judgment (Soroh did not die until very much later, and when the same matter is next discussed between Avrohom and Soroh she receives express and unequivocal Divine approval (21:12))? And how does this fit with the many rabbinic assertions that Soroh died without sin (see, in particular, Rashi on 23:1 and the Malbim on 23:3)? And in any event, the prohibition cited by the Baal Haturim is the prohibition in eulogising, but it is a letter of the word "and to cry for her", not of the word "to eulogise her" that is diminished.

An explanation designated expressly as a second alternative is sometimes so designated because it is indeed problematic but is nevertheless capable of teaching an important idea.

In this case, although it may be difficult or impossible for us to discern how or in what sense the point applied to Soroh, we can learn the general idea that it is both natural and acceptable for a person's conduct to affect my emotional reaction to what happens to him or her as a result of it. The reason for not eulogising someone who is directly responsible for his or her own death (and the halochoh applies only to direct responsibility) is that the responsibility changes the nature of our emotional response to the death from a relatively straight-forward sense of loss, that can be marked and to some extent alleviated by recounting the deceased's virtues, into something which may be more or less intense depending on the case but which in any event either is or should be more complicated.

Amnesty International this week published the results of a survey in which about 25 per cent of those who responded thought that victims of a certain crime are "partly to blame" for the crime if they have behaved in a manner that might objectively be thought to increase the risk of their being targeted. Amnesty describe the results as shocking.

I find the results disturbing not so much because they reveal malicious or wrong thinking but because they reveal confused thinking (on the part of those who compiled the survey as well as those who answered it). In particular, the results suggest that too many people fail to distinguish between their feelings about the perpetrator of a crime and their feelings about the victim.

The commission of a crime is always a moral wrong, of a greater or lesser degree depending on the nature of the crime and the mental and other circumstances of the criminal. The wilful murder of a person who stands already condemned to death is no less a murder. Theft is no less wrong because the victim behaved unattractively and unwisely by flaunting his or her wealth.

But what we feel about the victim, as distinct from what we feel about the criminal, will be affected by how he or she has behaved. The person who walks through a deprived area deliberately and ostentatiously displaying jewellery and other expensive accessories commits the wrong of placing a stumbling-block before the blind. His or her wrong does not excuse someone who then mugs him or her, and is not in itself a reason for treating the criminal more leniently. But it may, reasonably and constructively, affect how I feel about the victim and whether I feel the victim, and society in general, should have modified his or her behaviour.

If we are as a society troubled by the levels of crime of all kinds, our thoughts as to how crime can be reduced should be as broadly-ranging as possible; and we should be prepared to examine our own behaviour and consider whether, without offering it as an excuse for criminals, we could sensibly be doing more to reduce temptations to crime, both immediate and indirect, and to assist either actual or potential criminals to recover or retain proper paths of behaviour. To coin a phrase, "tough on crime and constructive on the causes of crime".

24

The End does not Justify the Means (1) – Anti-Terrorism

As a strong supporter of the State of Israel, I am proud that it is a rule of law state, with an effective Supreme Court which is designed to prevent abuses of all kinds. Set in a part of the world where torture is common-place, it is a particular source of pride that one of the most uncompromising judgments of the Supreme Court relates to the clear prohibition of the use of a range of interrogation techniques which were considered to amount to forms of torture. Torture in the field, in particular, must be humanly tempting as a method of increasing the effectiveness of interrogation, particularly where immediate intelligence is required in order to prevent bloodshed. But apart from the fact that torture is rarely if ever effective, it is inconsistent with maintaining the humanity of the State, which matters more than its continued existence. (From 2nd November 2005)

With much political attention being paid to anti-terrorist measures, two thoughts arising out of last week's parashah (I wanted to send this issue out last Friday but encountered technical problems) indicate the Jewish attitude on particular aspects of the issue.

Hashem creates people to rule over the natural world (Bereishis 1:26). Rashi points out that the word for to rule has an alternative possible root, the verb to go down. If humans are worthy, they will control the natural world. If not, they will descend beneath the level of the natural world and become controlled by it. We can use our intellect to use the natural resources of the world to perfect it for all. Or we can use our intellect to pursue individual self-gratification at the expense of others and become wholly controlled by the animal instincts inside us.

It is tempting to apply torture to terrorist prisoners (perhaps helpfully re-labelled as moderate forms of coercive punishment) in order to elicit information capable of saving innocent life. But to do so – or to allow other States in effect to do so on our behalf – is to lower ourselves to the level of the terrorist, allowing the end to justify the means. I have no right to depart from the path of rational, sensitive and humane treatment of prisoners, even in order to protect my own life or the lives of others. The Torah confers a right and duty to kill an attacker before he can kill me or someone else, but not to torture him or otherwise to indulge in behaviour which when we describe it as bestial we wrong the animal kingdom in ascribing to it what is in fact a purely human form of cruelty.

But there will be times when in order to protect innocent life I am obliged to do things which, while not inherently wrong or falling short of the standards required of humans created in the Divine image, nevertheless have undesirable consequences. The rabbis famously describe

Adam as having committed the first sin for the sake of heaven. What is meant is that the first sin is not to be understood in the same way as later sins. We sin by using the free-will gained when Adam ate from the tree of knowledge of good and evil in order to choose to gratify our animal selfishness rather than to serve Hashem by keeping His laws. Adam sinned by doing that which God had already predicted that Adam would do (as is clear from a careful reading of Bereishis 2:16 & 17) with the primary purpose of acquiring free-will which can be used to demonstrate love of the Divine attributes and thereby to serve Hashem as he has commanded, but which had the inevitable consequence that the same freedom would sometimes be abused, causing pain and suffering for the innocent victims throughout the world and throughout the centuries.

In Jewish thought, the end does not justify the means in the sense of enabling them to be disregarded or in the sense of making undesirable means inherently desirable. But we are required to be realistic, and to recognise that undesirable consequences will frequently flow from actions which are necessary in order to secure their primary purpose. When a terrorist is imprisoned, his or her family will suffer. When a terrorist is deported, he or she may suffer in the destination country (despite our compliance with our international obligations). These sufferings are not unimportant, nor are they to be in any sense welcomed as a form of deserved punishment: but they are to be accepted, with sensitivity, as the necessary and unavoidable consequences of taking reasonable and humane action to preserve the safety of the citizens for whom this country is responsible.

25

The Apprentice – Rewarding Deceit

Sometimes it seems as though all my rants are reserved for the religious community; and perhaps not unreasonably so, since if you present yourself and think of yourself as better than others you should at least aim not to fall too far below basic human standards of decency and morality. But occasionally I choose to allow myself to be equally concerned about the excesses of blatant and shameless secularism, particularly when it takes the form of a super-religious worship of money and material success, with an intensity that allows all means to be justified by the end of acquiring money. (From 11th June 2008)

In today's episode of *The Apprentice*, Alan Sugar chooses to hire the only contestant caught deliberately lying in his application form. Message to the nation: try lying – it's worth it: even if you get caught, nobody will care very much. Perhaps that's why the BBC showed *The Apprentice* after the Watershed – teaching children to lie is worse than teaching them to use bad language.

What chance is the United Kingdom today giving its youth, when the media celebrate and exalt those whose ideals, if they ever learned any, are constantly subjugated to their desire for transient success?

Even a child who aspires to succeed at a healthy, wholesome sport like running, sees one of the media's greatest sporting heroes – Paula Radcliffe – so desperate to win a marathon that she thinks it worth debasing herself to urinate in the gutter, while being filmed, rather than lose with dignity.

Alan Sugar makes no secret of being a Jew. What a shame that he cannot also demonstrate even a little of what it is to be Jewish. I am not talking about observance of the ritual laws, but about observance of the fundamental characteristics of the founders of our religion.

Abraham based our religion on kindness. *The Apprentice* is about getting on by putting other people down. The contestants are encouraged to fight in the boardroom as brutally as they can, having set each other up to fail so far as possible. When two of the contestants tried to bribe a shop-owner to ruin the other team's chances I thought they would have to go – how could Sugar be seen to countenance even the possibility of having such people in his business? One of them stayed.

Isaac developed the characteristic of strength. Strength in rabbinic understanding is the ability to control oneself. Single-minded determination to win at all costs is the opposite of strength: it is the weakness to allow ambition to prevail over principle. The contestants in *The Apprentice* seem to care only about winning: as one of them actually said, there is nothing he would not do to win: the extremity of weakness being portrayed as praiseworthy strength.

Jacob developed the characteristic of truth. Truth appears to count for little in Sugar's world. The winning contestant is the one who lied to get in; while one of the interviewers, proclaimed as a successful man of business, made light of this on the grounds that he had done it himself.

Many of us believe passionately that Judaism is not about social exclusivity, but about contributing to and being part of the real world. But that is difficult or impossible to do if the real world does not allow even basic standards of decent humanity to operate as the common denominator of acceptable behaviour.

26

Sharia Law in the United Kingdom

Mixing a religious and a secular perspective is notoriously difficult. Jewish law should make it relatively safe, because in most matters monetary the Jewish law defers to and imports the secular law (particularly where there is a contract reflecting local commercial practice) and the Beis Din ought not to assert or accept any jurisdiction in non-monetary matters. But it's not always as simple as that in practice ... (From 7th February 2008)

The Archbishop of Canterbury said today that it might be helpful in a number of ways to permit the application of Sharia law in the United Kingdom: "There's a place for finding what would be a constructive accommodation with some aspects of Muslim law, as we already do with some other aspects of religious law".

Jewish thought and practice has always believed that religious law can and must work alongside that of our host nations.

On the one hand, we have a concept of *dina d'malchuso dina hi* – the law of the land has status in

Jewish law. The rule of secular law is vital for the well-being of all those who live in secular societies, since the religious communal institutions are (except in a country wholly governed by and in accordance with those institutions) unable both theoretically and practically to provide effective control over most aspects of human behaviour. The establishment of a just and fair system of secular law is one of the Noachide laws, an obligation on all non-Jewish states, and one which we who live in those states are therefore bound to support by compliance and respect.

On the other hand, there are some matters of communal law that can be enforced effectively only within the communal religious institutions. English secular law has long granted autonomy to the Jewish community in matters of kashrus and marriage, and with occasional forays into the secular legal institutions for the resolution of disputes the system appears to work to the satisfaction of all.

Between these two areas lies a wide range of civil matters where the secular institutions may well be able to handle them, but where there may be significant advantages in having them addressed by people who are able to empathise with the social, cultural and religious aspirations and values of the parties involved. One takes it that this is one of the areas to which the Archbishop is referring. Certainly Jewish law strongly supports the idea that a dispute between Jews should be handled by the Jewish courts wherever possible (Shemos 21:1 ; Gittin 88b). And in the United Kingdom for some years we have managed to put this into practice through the mechanism of the Arbitration Acts: Jews with a dispute on any commercial matter can go the

Beis Din and sign an arbitration agreement, following which the matter proceeds as an arbitration and the Beis Din's decision may be enforced if necessary through the secular courts, and can be challenged there only on limited, mostly procedural, grounds.

An important point about the latter process is that it does not involve imposing Jewish law on anyone who chooses not to be bound by it; it makes it possible for those who wish to have disputes determined in accordance with religious values that they share to go to their religious judges and have the matter treated accordingly (although, as I say above, that will often involve the importation of principles of local secular law, as a matter of *dina d'malchuso dina hi*).

27

Publish and Damn –
Trial by Jewish Chronicle

Anonymity for those charged with, but not convicted of, an offence is a controversial and complicated issue in criminal law. Anonymity for alleged victims and publicity for alleged perpetrators can seem clearly unfair; but controlled publicity is sometimes essential to encourage sufficient victims or witnesses to come forward to secure a conviction. Sheer prurient speculation is, however, clearly and grotesquely wrong. One would hope that anything calling itself a Jewish newspaper in any sense of the term would be careful: one would hope ... (From 14th June 2008)

One might hope for high standards of journalism from *The Jewish Chronicle*, or at least basic observance of the Jewish laws of permitted and non-permitted speech.

In this week's issue, *the Jewish Chronicle* reports that a man has been charged with a very serious sexual offence. The man is named and enough details given of the case to be likely to cause him to be stigmatised by many who read the article. He is accused by a boy, whose name is not given for legal reasons.

For all *the Jewish Chronicle* can possibly know, this charge may be a complete fabrication. Stranger things have happened. The man may be acquitted when tried, or the charge may even be dropped before that. Yet the stain of the accusation in the eyes of the prejudiced will follow him to the grave: thanks to *the Jewish Chronicle*.

In Jewish law, there is no excuse for the publication of what is presently an unsubstantiated accusation – to do so is mere loshon horoh – culpable gossip.

Of course, there are occasions when the public or a section of it requires to be warned about a danger even in the absence of a conviction: but this would not be the way to secure that end, which requires to be achieved with care, sensitivity and judgment.

28

Innocent or Mostly Innocent?

Separation of executive and judicial power is a key feature of the rule of law; Jewish thought has always stressed the importance of the distinction. (From 19th June 2005)

In a recent criminal trial in America attracting considerable media interest, the defendant was acquitted; but his acquittal was accompanied by some public speculation that he may have been guilty of offences despite the fact that the prosecution had failed to prove its case in respect of the charges preferred.

The Jewish approach to a situation like this is clear.

The secular rule against double jeopardy, a person being tried more than once for the same crime, is found, but with variations, in Jewish law. In particular, while we will always reopen a criminal matter to turn a guilty verdict into an acquittal, we will not reopen an acquittal.

Once a person's acquittal is recorded, he must be allowed to function, in the same way as any other person, without aspersions being cast against him extra-judicially and in a manner which carries neither accountability or responsibility. So a former juror, or any other person, who accuses an acquitted defendant of wrong-doing is exposed to the same potential liability in Jewish law for defamation, and has to abide by the same laws of permitted speech, as apply in relation to anyone else.

However, it can of course in theory happen that a defendant is acquitted for technical reasons, while the court is satisfied beyond doubt that he was guilty of a crime. In secular law, for example, there can be technical reasons for the inadmissibility of evidence whose veracity nobody doubts. And in Jewish law there may, for example, be a family relationship between the only two available witnesses which prevents the evidence of both being admitted; or there may have been a deficiency in the terms in which the requisite warning was administered.

In such a case, Jewish law allows the court to impose whatever measures – including imprisonment – it considers necessary for the protection of society. Anyone who believes that the verdict may leave unanswered questions of public safety is therefore able to apply to the courts for relief: but not to indulge in private extra-judicial accusations.

In this way, the Torah gives unlimited powers to the judicial institutions to preserve the rule of law and to protect the public, while at the same time ensuring that individuals have their liberty and reputation protected from interference otherwise than in accordance with due judicial process.

29

Small Claims Beis Din

The purity of the rule of law is the essence of Jewish thought and law, and it rejects any correlation between the monetary value of a claim and the amount of care needed to determine it. That this is a fundamental principle of Jewish law is confirmed by rabbinic exposition of the discussion between Moses and Jethro when the latter urges the necessity of establishing a judicial hierarchy for the efficient and effective dispensation of justice. I just wish more modern rabbis would remember the fundamental principles of Jewish thought ...
(From 7th January 2017)

A UK Beis Din (rabbinic court) has just announced a new small claims service for claims between £500 and £5000 where both parties choose to use it; the guarantee is that they will "receive a brief, written, binding psak within 72 hours".

I must be missing something.

It's great that a Beis Din is promising a swift decision: one of the embarrassing features of the Beis Din system in this country is how long cases are sometimes allowed to drag on.

But what's that got to do with the value of the claim?

Everybody knows that the complexity of a claim and its value do not necessarily correlate.

In secular courts, there are a number of practical reasons why small claims are provided with a range of faster tracks.

A Beis Din is meant to do one of two things: (a) determine a compromise; or (b) decide the truth of liability.

There is no reason why either of those should be quicker with a "small" claim (and which part of the community is the Beis Din prioritising if it considers £5,000 a "small" claim?).

The speed of the resolution should be determined by the complexity of the case, not its value.

Instead of offering a service that equates complexity with value and thereby inevitably risks giving decisions that are poorly thought out in order to meet an artificial 72-hour deadline, all Botei Din should concentrate on treating all cases as urgent, and providing answers as quickly as is consistent with the search for Torah justice.

If the parties don't care whether a decision is right or wrong but just want it quickly because the claim isn't big enough to matter much to either of them, they'd do better tossing a coin.

30

Speed Camera Detectors

My normal anti-gambling rant is pretty muted when it comes to a simple prize raffle for charity; but they still need to exercise a modicum of common sense when choosing the prizes ... (From 27th July 2005)

On a previous occasion I outlined the Torah objections to high-prize raffles being used by charities. The Side-by-Side charity, an enormously worthy charity that works with children who have special needs, runs an annual multi-option raffle known as a Chinese Auction. Looking at this year's list of prizes I found something that horrified me even more than the basic concept of exploiting human greed to raise money for charity.

Raffle 13 is for a "GPS Snooper Safety Alert System". The caption to the prize is "Don't get caught by that speed camera – don't be tricked, be one step ahead". The detector is advertised as providing "advance warning of police speed traps, accident blackspots, speed cameras, schools, hazardous and dangerous situations on the road".

There is only one reason for warning people that they are approaching speed traps or cameras: to enable them to speed without being caught.

A number of aspects of Torah law are engaged by this device. First, it is against English law to aid and abet the commission of an offence. Facilitating speeding is aiding the commission of an offence and is therefore unlawful. Supplying the detector is part of the facilitation, and is also unlawful. Torah law requires us to abide by the law of our host community – the dina d'malchuto – and the provision of this prize is therefore contrary to English law and halachah.

Secondly, speeding itself is dangerous, and is therefore contrary to the Torah requirement to protect one's own health.

Thirdly, speeding poses a known and statistically significant threat to the lives of others: therefore, if a person speeds and kills or injures others he will be culpable in halochoh both in the civil sense as a mazik (tortfeasor) and as having neglected the injunction to care for others as for oneself.

Fourthly, the Jewish equivalent of part of the prohibition of aiding and abetting an offence is the prohibition against putting a stumbling block before the blind: by providing this detector one supports and encourages those who are too stupid or wicked to see the importance of not driving dangerously.

How appalling that a charity dedicated to the wonderful work of supporting children with physical and mental disabilities should have, in a moment's uncharacteristic thoughtlessness, caused itself to assist one of the crimes that is most responsible for causing death and injury to children and adults in England today.

JEWISH COMMUNITY

31

Rabbi Dovid Cooper o'h

According to Talmudic tradition, at any one time there are 36 completely righteous people in the world by whose merit it is permitted to continue to exist. However literal or allegorical one likes to consider this statement, it is certainly true that there are a few people whose purity is both inspiring and seemingly complete. And the ability to recognise and be inspired by people who are spiritually exemplary is as important as it is to be able to withstand the influence of fraudsters and crooks who pretend to be spiritual for their own personal gain. The very short appreciation that I wrote below about Rabbi Cooper shortly after his death probably needs nothing added to it now by me. It is important to me to be able to record, however, that members of his family contacted me after I first published this appreciation online and expressed their approval of it as an appropriate reflection. (From 23rd April 2010)

Today sees the end of the shiva after the death last shabbos of Rabbi Dovid Cooper o'h, former Rav of North Hendon Adas Yisroel.

This week's parashah is a double parashah: acharei mos-kedoshim. For most people, kedushah comes only "acharei mos" (sanctity comes only after death).

All of us who knew Rabbi Cooper z'l even very slightly were in no doubt that we stood in the presence of a rare example of a living kedushah, which constantly inspired us: we came away from talking to him with a wish to do better.

For much of his life his mind was of an extremely rare acuity: as his intellectual faculties diminished, the purity and elevation of his character were simply thrown into sharper relief. We saw that genius belongs to this world, but its application to learning for the sake of Heaven refines the soul to a degree that, again, inspired us all.

Above all, Rabbi Cooper z'l taught me the beauty of simplicity. Although his mind was capable of impressive feats of intellectual gymnastics, he did not indulge in rhetoric for its own sake, nor did he cultivate charisma. He said what had to be said in a straightforward way. He applied Torah rigidly, but his understanding of Torah included an appreciation of sensitivity and humanity. Honesty and yashrus ("we bend over backwards, but we don't break") are commodities of which the world stands in much need: may his memory inspire us all to do a little better.

32

Boruch Dayan Ho'Emes-Dayan Gershon Lopian Z'tzl

Most of my posts on The Sceptic Blog *are greeted by an adoring public with a total silence which I have always quite reasonably interpreted as unqualified approbation. It was no surprise to me that comments were posted about this particular piece. I remember vividly writing it in my office at my parents' home immediately after I heard the news that Dayan Lopian had died: the words flowed onto the screen, and I had no doubt at the time that I was reflecting what many thousands of people around the world were thinking. Two of the comments made a particular impression: one because it came from a family who were particularly close to the Dayan and who said they had found the post helpful in encapsulating their feelings; and the other because it came from a mother who said her six-year-old daughter had already asked her "Mummy, who will we ask our questions to now?" The feeling of loss has not diminished over time: in fact, it has intensified as we have all found it impossible to find anyone to fill the void. Yehi zichro boruch. (From 30th January 2014)*

I once heard that the more effort a person takes to conceal his or her greatness in this world, the wider the Gates of Heaven are thrown open for them b'yom haDin.

The Gates of Heaven are opened wide tonight.

The Dayan spent more effort than most people spend in pushing themselves forward in keeping himself back. He shrank from honour, from controversy, from ambition, from everything that is Moitzi es Ho'Odom Min Ho'Olom. For his part, he could have gone unrecognised and unknown and been perfectly happy; which is why he was known and sought after from every corner of the world, why his telephone never stopped ringing, and why he will be irreplaceable.

From the Dayan, one could learn ahavas habrios. He loved every human being. He loved the weak, the broken, the silly and the ineffectual; and he even loved those who didn't think they were any of those things. He had time for us all. His 'phone number was on Directory Enquiries for all to see: and he answered his own 'phone – you didn't have to pluck up courage to get through a wall of secretaries or to explain your business; if you needed an ear and an answer, you got both.

From the Dayan, one could learn sholom. He was always interested in people – but he was never interested in taking sides, or leading or supporting battles for anything. His infectious smile and laughter dissolved discord and united people in ahavas haTorah.

From the Dayan, one could learn emes. He was afraid of nothing and nobody. If something was nonsense you were told it was nonsense. If something was wrong, no amount of discussion would make it right; and if it was right, no amount of pressure would make it wrong.

Boruch Dayan HoEmes.

33

Ronite Bitton

*Child abduction cases are not uncommon within the
Orthodox Jewish community. Or, perhaps, it would be
more accurate to say that they are not uncommon in
families where one partner has either decided to leave or
decided to join the Orthodox Jewish community.
Emotions and tempers run high, and abduction is commonly used either as a way of ensuring that the child
remains within an orthodox environment, or as a means
of protecting the child from what are seen as unhealthy
orthodox influences. Because of the international nature
of the Jewish community, international abduction is
quite common, with its corresponding complications. Of
course, every situation has to be approached on its own
terms and in its own context. Secular law in the United
Kingdom has only relatively recently established the
welfare of the child as the paramount consideration in
all family proceedings, with the passage of the Children
Act 1989. The Jewish community could do with reas-
serting this principle in its own approach to dealings
with children in breakdown cases that cross international borders. While some orthodox communities take
it as axiomatic that depriving a child of an orthodox*

upbringing is inevitably the worst possible outcome for the child's welfare, and while antagonistic anti-religious groups take the opposite position, it is likely that the real welfare of real children will continue to be disregarded if they are treated as shuttlecocks in a game of religious badminton. I never found out the truth of the factors in the case touched on in the piece below; like the Halpern case (see Chapter 18), it caused a brief flurry which has been allowed to subside so as not to disturb our complacent conviction that all is well with the Jewish community. (From 1st June 2012)

I was asked to write something about the case of Ronite Bitton.

Details of her case are already available on the internet. In essence, she is facing a lengthy term of imprisonment, in addition to terms already served, because she is accused of having removed her son to Israel and arranged for him to disappear, in order to avoid the possibility of his being ordered to return to live with his father in Belgium.

There are plenty of impassioned pleas and opinions about the case in various places on the internet. I am not going to add to their number: apart from anything, I have had no opportunity to check the truth of any of the factual assertions made in the case.

Whatever the facts, considering the case can serve as a reminder that the Hague Convention on International Child Abduction can be a two-edged sword. The Convention was designed as a tool against injustice and a way of imposing rule of law among the 80 or so signatory countries. A fantastic idea: to protect children from being dragged from one country to another in order to evade justice or to frustrate orders of courts made with their welfare in mind.

But all legal systems can go wrong: and what happens if one legal system, whether through corruption or incompetence, threatens to destroy a child's life? Like diplomatic immunity or extradition, the only way the Convention system can operate is by unquestioning respect by each participant for each other participant's processes, even in cases where they seem to have miscarried. As soon as you allow a participant to examine the quality of justice in a particular case, the system starts to break down and to become infected by political and other considerations.

So can the Convention be used to enforce injustice? Yes, of course it can.

If some of the assertions made on Ronite's behalf are true, she has been the victim both of this inflexibility of the Convention, and also of actual injustices and failures within the Israeli judicial system.

In the United Kingdom, there is now a Criminal Cases Review Commission, which is able to review criminal cases independently and, if they believe that justice may have miscarried, instigate fresh proceedings. Perhaps the Convention needs to have a similar system on an international scale so that, without compromising the automatic nature of the Convention as a general rule, there is a non-political and independent way of intervening in cases where the Convention appears to have been used as a weapon of injustice, whether through corruption or incompetence. I have a troubled feeling that if such a body were to exist it would find more than enough cases to occupy it.

In the meantime, I would encourage anyone who feels strongly about injustice to access some of the petition and other sites about this particular case, to satisfy themselves as to the facts, and then to take any action they feel inclined to take, whether by signing a petition or otherwise publicising the case. A forgotten injustice will never be rectified: a publicised one just may be.

34

Rabbis Gone Wrong –
Tisha B'Av 2009

I have always been attracted to the idea of fighting losing battles; and I have probably picked none that appears more hopeless than to urge rabbis around the world to do something to produce an effective system of self-regulation so that the title rabbi becomes at least in general more synonymous with spiritual inspiration than with a tendency towards facilitating money-laundering. Like many who fight losing battles, I have a tendency to exaggerate: not all rabbis are money laun-derers, and one would like to think that only a minority of them are susceptible to involvement in such matters (although, taking those who assume the title rabbi worldwide all round, I feel the minority would be rather more sizeable than one would wish). But saying most rabbis are not crooks should not be enough for any self-respecting profession. Lawyers are well aware that many of their number are crooked, and they take steps to provide methods of self-regulation and procedures for having complaints against lawyers effectively deter-mined and appropriate remedies, including expulsion, applied. There is no equivalent in relation to the worldwide rabbinate, nor are there any serious attempts to create one. At an event about the state of the rabbinate held in United Synagogue Alei Tzion in Hendon a few years ago, I shared a panel with Dayan Lichtenstein and Rabbi Michael Pollock. Rabbi Pollock, in a praiseworthy attempt to preserve the peace when matters were getting a little bit heated, made the pacific comment that we could, after all, all agree that by and large the rabbis do a good job. Rather to his dismay, I suspect, I responded that while I applauded the peace-loving sentiments behind his proposition, I simply didn't feel it was true: on the whole, our rabbis do a mediocre job. The fact that we tend to praise them lavishly when they provide anything like value for money in communal service, is perhaps more our fault than theirs, and inevitably tends to lead to complacency on their part and a lack of desire to push themselves. How often do I hear someone saying of a full-time communal rabbi: "he's so wonderful he came to visit me in hospital"; and rather meanly and cynically think to myself: "pay me a salary rather larger than I would be likely to command in any other profession open to me, and I will come and visit you in hospital as well". Outright cynicism of this kind is perhaps not to be encouraged; but nor are the rabbis to be encouraged to think that on the whole worldwide they as a group are doing a good job. They are not. And their apparent insouciance at that fact is one of the most troubling aspects of institutional Judaism today. (From 24th July 2009)

Let's prepare for the worst – that not every one of the rabbis arrested by the FBI yesterday turns out to be a maligned innocent, but that rabbis turn out to have knowingly been involved in money laundering.

If that is the case, then here is this year's Kamtza and Bar Kamtza challenge for the rabbinical world and the whole Jewish community, just in time for this year's Tisha B'av.

If I call myself a Jew and I behave badly, God's name is besmirched. If I call myself a rabbi and behave badly, the Torah is discredited: thousands of neshomos may be turned away from Jewish values and practice because the Judaism that a "rabbi" represents appears spiritually bankrupt.

One of the many faults of this generation's Jewish community is that we have allowed people too easily to assume the title Rabbi. On the one hand, semichah has become a kind of routine examination whereby people can obtain official ordination after just a few years' study and without any serious kind of estimation of their moral character or leadership qualities. On the other hand, even without semichah of any formal kind people are allowed to assume the title, or are accorded it as an honorific, without any serious justification or need. (The Chazon Ish did not have semichah, because he never needed it.)

To reverse this process would be enormously difficult. But not impossible, if the will from the rabbis and the people were there. The essence of the Kamtza and Bar Kamtzah story is that the rabbis sat and did nothing. The rabbis, with our encouragement and support, need to restore the lustre to their holy office. They need publicly to expel those who degrade it, by public proclamations of who is no longer fitting to act in reliance on a semichah; and they need to take serious steps to ensure that worldwide the title is reserved for those who have shown more than a few years' attendance at a Talmudic sausage factory to deserve it

35

Another Rabbi goes to prison – no news there ...

Trust in the rabbis is a fundamental component of institutionalised Judaism. But what happens when it becomes difficult or even impossible to find any rabbis worth trusting? Is that the end of the religion? On the contrary: it may be the end of institutionalised Judaism as transmitted to Moses on Mount Sinai, but that merely throws us back to an earlier and purer form of Judaism, a personal and individual covenant between each person and his or her conception of God, as taught by Abraham and Sarah. (From 7th January 2017)

The really depressing thing about the reports that former Israeli Chief Rabbi Yona Metzger is to plead guilty to corruption charges in a plea bargain is how completely un-shocking the reports are.

I don't suppose anybody is surprised that an Israeli Chief Rabbi was prepared to take bribes.

How shocking is it that it's no longer shocking?

Never mind – let's just keep repeating the mantra Mi K'Amcho Yisroel and not worry about the real world ...

Sometimes it seems that almost every large Jewish religious institution around the world is beset by scandals of corruption and abuse.

Perhaps that means that individual Jews need to become completely self-reliant for recognising and applying Jewish values in their own daily lives, and cannot expect to get much in the way of reliable guidance from anybody else.

And perhaps that's no bad thing ...

36

Clarifying Jewish Orthodoxy by Disowning Murderers and Paedophiles

Religious communities acquire a responsibility to regulate themselves. It's all too easy just to disclaim responsibility by shrugging our shoulders and saying, "that's not a real Jew", "that's not a real Christian", "that's not a real Buddhist", "that's not a real Muslim" – if the wider religious community does nothing to expel or control rogues, we become complicit in their roguery. (From 2nd August 2015)

The vicious and depraved lunatic Yishai Schlissel who murdered a marcher on the Gay Pride event in Jerusalem is described in the press – not unreasonably given his appearances and pretensions – as "an ultra-Orthodox Jew".

The chillingly sane child-abuser Todros Grynhaus is similarly described for similar reasons.

Grynhaus' Counsel told the judge in court that "Part of the punishment for this man is of course the shame and exposure and social ostracisation within his own community".

So far, that is, of course, unhappily not true. The only people who have been shamed, exposed and ostracised are the victims.

Orthodox Judaism needs to act fast and decisively. Unless we all act together both to proclaim that violence and abuse are incompatible with orthodox Jewish observance and show by the community's actions that knowledge, zeal and money will not be reasons to acknowledge murderers and paedophiles as part of our community, then we will be rightly tainted as a community in the eyes of the world.

Community is about membership with rules. If the rules of the Jewish orthodox community are not effective to protect the vulnerable and to enforce basic standards of human decency, it will no longer be morally tolerable to be seen to identify with it.

37

Neo-Nazi Demonstration in Golders Green

While we continue to attract the animosity of horrible people, we can't be doing everything wrong ... (From 25ᵗʰ June 2015)

The Neo-Nazis who are proposing to hold a demonstration in Golders Green this coming Saturday have chosen well.

The timing is good: we are approaching the three weeks, culminating in the 9th of Av, when we commemorate Jewish persecutions throughout the ages, and remind ourselves that our enemies are (unwitting) messengers of God from whose actions we need to learn something.

And the content of the demonstration is good: they propose to burn copies of the Talmud and Israeli flags. The Talmud contains and represents the whole of Jewish ritual, and the land of Israel provides and represents Jewish physical security.

On Saturday, as the Neo-Nazis burn the Talmud and the Flag, I will take this as an important reminder of the need to ensure that my Jewish belief is internal and self-reliant. It is about my personal relationship with God, based on Abraham's teachings of recognising a single Creator and being inspired by that recognition to serve Him through kindness to others.

It is easy to become too reliant on religious ritual for our spiritual habits, and to become too trusting in the State of Israel for our national physical security. The Neo-Nazis will remind us that both of these are fragile, and that neither of them is what matters.

As the old liturgical poem has it: "I will build a sanctuary in my heart" – nobody can destroy that.

38

Limmud – A Plea
for Intolerance

It took a long time for me to stop feeling guilty for looking on reform and other forms of progressive Judaism as not being "real" Judaism. As an opinion, it is clearly bigoted; and if reform and other adherents choose to regard it as condescending and patronising, then perhaps it is. But it is as much my right to believe that my version of Judaism is the only authentic one as it is someone else's to disagree. Theological flexibility and tolerance has never been a mark of Judaism – "For I am a jealous God ...". (From 10th November 2013)

As the date for this year's Limmud Conference draws nearer, the Jewish community is able to put aside the distracting trivialities of past months – minor irritations like discovering that the rabbinate is completely unable to provide an effective system for investigating allegations of sexual abuse by rabbis – and concentrate on the all-important task of infighting.

The Limmud controversy is enlivened this year by two novelties. First, the new Chief Rabbi Mirvis has publicly announced his intention of attending. Secondly, in response, letters have been published by orthodox rabbis denouncing the event.

The fact that Chief Rabbi Mirvis has decided to go is hardly startling. Since he opened his term of office by declaring his wish to act for all kinds of Judaism – progressive as well as orthodox – he would have lost every shred of credibility that declaration carried had he refused to attend the main pluralist and inclusive event in the communal calendar. Nor does it require particular courage: it will make no difference to the chareidi community's attitude to his chief rabbinate – when it suits them they will use him and when it doesn't they won't. (It probably won't make any real difference to the progressive communities' attitudes to him either; they will pocket the gesture and demand more, pushing him beyond wherever he draws his boundaries in order to assert their need for separate recognition by the secular authorities.)

The letters of condemnation are pretty futile too. With one exception, those that I have seen are very much in the "preaching to the converted style", and do not even pretend to argue in a way that will convince anyone who needs convincing. The one exception is a modern orthodox Rabbi who has written a brilliant description of his personal attitudes to the event.

The battle – trivial, parochial and communally-self-absorbed as it is – has of course been lost years ago. Outside Chareidi circles, it has long been regarded as intolerant and bigoted to object to Limmud.

So perhaps this is a reasonable time to remember that Judaism has always been, theologically speaking, intolerant and bigoted. In human terms, Jews have always been

– if they follow their religion – generous, humble and unlimitedly tolerant in their dealings with Jews and non-Jews alike. In theological terms, there is no room in orthodox Judaism for compromise, or for acceptance that any other religion or version of religion has any truth that is not also found in orthodox Judaism itself.

It is this theological intolerance that would lead many orthodox Jews to feel uncomfortable at an event that has pluralism and the acceptance of pluralism at its heart. They like their educational events to take place in an atmosphere of respect for orthodoxy as the only authentic version of Judaism. The presence of progressive educators being presented as equally valid sources of education and inspiration as orthodox rabbis would be enough to make many orthodox Jews feel profoundly uncomfortable.

All very bigoted and intolerant: but I wonder if the spirit of tolerance and generosity that prevails at Limmud (or so I am told) can find room to feel tolerant and generous spirited towards those of us who stay away because we genuinely believe that our religion requires us to be bigoted and intolerant? (Or is it, perhaps, infected with an intolerance and inverted bigotry of its very own?)

39

Knocking the
Rabbis ... into Shape

I wonder if in history it has always been the generations that most needed strong rabbis that have mainly had weak ones. (From 6ᵗʰ August 2013)

A couple of weeks ago I had the pleasure of taking part in a Shabbos afternoon panel at Alei Tzion shul in Hendon, chaired by its Rabbi Daniel Roselaar, and consisting of Dayan Lichtenstein, Rabbi Michael Pollack and myself. The subject was whether rabbinic authority is damaged beyond repair by recent events in the UK, Israel and America.

You can see an account of the discussion here: http://youandus.theus.org.uk/communities-focus/alei-tzion-hosts-summer-debate-rabbinic-authority-in-the-21st-century-damaged-beyond-repair/.

I see from that account that I called for an independent regulatory body to work across all Botei Din.

And so I did; the idea had been waffling around in my mind for some time, but the event somehow crystallised it into a simple thought.

The catalyst was something that Rabbi Pollack said: in a helpful attempt to keep the event peaceful and constructive he observed that most rabbis of course do a good job. In an unhelpful attempt to keep the event provocative and constructive I disagreed, and said that by and large our rabbis do a fairly mediocre job, and that we have come to expect so little from them that our expectations are easily exceeded by very moderate performance.

How often is a rabbi commended as wonderful for having visited a parishioner in hospital when that is no more than precisely what he is paid a hefty salary for doing? I am all in favour of rabbis and other workers being commended for performing beyond the call of duty, but that should be tested against a reasonably exacting and challenging initial threshold of what that duty should be.

We do have some wonderful and inspiring rabbis in the UK community today; and we have very few really bad ones; but we have a fair number of unimpressively mediocre ones; and with the system as it stands there is little impetus for them to strive to improve themselves as a profession.

Recent events have shown the lack of a disciplinary body, such as other professions have, for dealing with misconduct by rabbis that is not, or may not be, criminal in nature. But on reflection I see that there is an equal need for a body that can deal with issues that are not about misconduct, but merely poor performance (along the lines of the Medical Professional Performance Act that I drafted in 1995).

The more I think about the idea, the more useful I think it could be; and it really need not be very complicated to establish.

We need a group of communal activists who are prepared to act as an unpaid disciplinary body for rabbis, including a chair with experience in employment law and a panel of unpaid rabbinic advisers. Hopefully nobody would be called on to act very often, and the body could sit in separate panels (as do many professional regulatory bodies) each consisting of perhaps one person with employment law experience and two or three lay-members, with a rabbi in a purely advisory capacity.

Complaints about poor performance and misconduct could be referred to this body in accordance with its rules.

Now comes the simple bit – every new contract offered by any congregation would include a clause providing for all complaints about poor performance or misconduct to be considered by the disciplinary body in accordance with its rules. The rabbi and the employing organization would agree to be bound by the body's decisions.

There are one or two more details that might need to be thought through – but that is the essence. (Halachic enforcement considerations are significant but not insurmountable.)

One result would be to provide real protection for the community from misconduct and inefficiency by rabbis – much more importantly, however, the system could serve as the basis for new professional standards that rabbis could set for themselves, and therefore as a mechanism for restoring trust in, and the moral authority of, the profession that is meant to be the backbone of our religion.

40

North Hendon Adath Yisroel – Time to Leave the Union of Orthodox Hebrew Congregations

I was so proud of my fellow congregants when we stood up to authority and expressed our contempt of a spiritually bankrupt institution in the only way possible, by leaving it. (From 31st December 2012)

Tomorrow morning iy'h the North Hendon Adath Yisroel Synagogue will hold an Extraordinary General Meeting to decide whether or not to leave the UOHC.

I hope and pray that we do leave, if only for the selfish reason that then I will be able to return and daven in my local shul to which I have belonged for about 20 years. For the last two weeks, I have felt unable to set foot inside the building, and this post explains why.

Abuse of the vulnerable is a natural human temptation, and it is therefore inevitable that in any community someone will sooner or later be abused by someone else.

The test of a community is not whether it can prevent abuse, but how it handles abuse when it happens or is alleged.

Indian society today is having to take a long and painful look at itself to work out how it has allowed attitudes to women to deteriorate to such a degree that abusive and violent treatment of women had become so commonplace that the atrocity that occurred a few days ago was simply waiting to happen (or had already happened further from the public, and international, eye).

Catholic society around the world has been having to take a long and painful look at itself for some time to work out how child abuse had become, in effect, tolerated and condoned by a religious institution.

Until very recently, many orthodox Jews may have had our fears that perhaps abuse – which must inevitably occasionally happen in our community since we are as susceptible to human failings as any other community – may not have been being handled properly. But I for one have not felt it necessary to confront these fears openly and investigate them – perhaps I should have done, but to look the other way is another strong human temptation.

In the words of one of the most powerful activism songs of all time, "How many ears must one man have, before he can hear people cry? ... How many times can a man turn his head, pretending he just doesn't see?".

The crying is now too loud to pretend not to hear it; and to turn one's head in today's situation makes one morally complicit in what is happening.

The Torah law of sexual offences makes an important distinction. Where a woman has an adulterous relationship in a populated area, she is unable in effect to plead that she was forced because the Torah asks why she did not cry out; in the countryside, however, the Torah plaintively notes "maybe she did cry out and there was nobody to hear", and expands that maybe she did not cry out only because she knew there was nobody there.

The women of India had almost given up crying out at the degrading treatment to which many of them are treated every day, because they feared that in one of the most densely populated areas of the world there was still nobody who cared to hear them: they have just found new voice, and one hopes and prays that the ears of all Indian society will listen.

The vulnerable of the London orthodox Jewish community have apparently just cried out. A number of specific allegations of abuse have been made against one of the most powerful and respected Rabbis of the community. I am not required or able to pass judgment on whether these allegations are true or false: but as a member of the community I am morally obliged to satisfy myself that the cries of the vulnerable are listened to in an appropriate way.

There is only one appropriate way to listen to allegations of abuse in our community. Our botei din have no criminal jurisdiction; so in any matter of law that is not confined to a dispute between individuals about property matters that can be arbitrated under the Arbitration Act 1996, we are obliged both as a matter of halacha and as a matter of secular law to present evidence of any alleged crime to the police, and evidence of any other kind of abuse of the vulnerable to appropriate civil authorities (such as the social services).

If we believe that perhaps an allegation of abuse may not amount to an allegation of a criminal offence, whether because the acts complained of may have been consensual or for any other reason, we need to leave it to the police and the prosecuting authorities to look at the evidence and make a decision. It is not for us to decide, for example, whether apparent consent is vitiated by having been obtained through undue influence or through fraudulent misrepresentations as to the halachic position; those are matters on which we could only speculate but the prosecuting authorities first, and possibly later the courts, are equipped and obliged to decide.

If we are to be a God-fearing community, our self-regulation must be efficient and effective, and it must know its limitations and engage with those outside people and authorities who are available to take over where self-regulation is no longer available.

The only proper response to anyone who comes to a rabbi with an allegation of having been abused is "get in my car and I will take you to the police station, I will stay with you while you make a statement to the police, and I will support to my last breath your right and duty to have your allegation investigated by the authorities of the State, so that wrong-doers can be punished and deterred, and other vulnerable people can be protected".

Members of our self-absorbed and insular community will of course be very reluctant to go to the police. It is never easy or pleasant for someone to make a complaint about a sexual offence. But many women, children and men have found the courage to go through the traumas of the court procedures, at horrendous personal emotional cost, in order to make sense of what has happened to them by using it to prevent the same from happening to others. Members of our community may have additional fears for themselves and their families: but outspoken support from the rabbis acting together can allay those fears, and if they do not provide that support then they do not deserve to be our rabbis.

The fear of washing dirty linen in public is something I have never been able to understand. Dirty linen smells: to pretend there is no dirty linen in the cupboard deceives nobody. And why go through the charade of a pointless pretence anyway? It is no disgrace for one's linen to get dirty: but it is a disgrace not to take it to the wash in the same way as everybody else.

To encourage people not to take criminal allegations to the criminal authorities, or to encourage them to use alternative, necessarily ineffective methods of "resolving" potentially criminal matters, rests on a failure to understand the halachic implications of the law of mesirah[12] as it applies in the context of the political and legal structures of the United Kingdom today. The Torah forbids recourse to the secular courts in matters where a Beis Din is competent; and it forbids recourse even in other matters to an arbitrary, unjust and inherently anti-semitic system. There are no Cossacks in the UK today; and although the police and courts are not perfect, and miscarriages of justice will occur, there are mechanisms for righting even those; and they are not as inevitable to begin with as the injustice that is bound to occur when criminal allegations are dealt with in an informal manner by people who are neither trained nor appointed to assess them, nor have effective remedies to deal with them.

"Leave the rabbis to sort this out – we can make the place too hot to hold any perpetrators", as well

---

[12] Handing fellow-Jews over to secular (normally arbitrary and anti-semitic) authorities.

as resting on this halachic misconception, can result only either in perverts being shunted from place to place to reoffend once people's short memories have become confused with the passage of time, or in innocent people being driven from their homes and their livelihoods based on insufficiently tested evidence. This behaviour is not only wilfully ineffective, but may, depending on the precise circumstances, amount to the criminal offence of conspiracy to pervert the course of justice.

As for behaviour which after full analysis of the available evidence, and full cooperation from the community, the police or the Crown Prosecution Service decide is not criminal, or is not sufficiently evidenced to make a conviction likely, at that point the question of self-regulation arises again. The rabbis need to have, as do the medical and other professions, a process for dealing with allegations of professional impropriety not involving (or not necessarily involving) criminality. That procedure needs to be transparent and efficient, following due process in an accountable and public way (subject to such privacy as is justified in individual cases for publicly recorded reasons); and it needs to engage effective and proportionate remedies.

I can happily belong to a community in which I am not the only imperfect human being; I cannot belong to a community in which my silence is part of the collective cowardice and institutional inertia that allows the cries of the vulnerable to go unheard.

North Hendon has always been a remarkable community. If nothing demogs like demography, in the same way few things geog like geography: as a result of being set a little apart physically from the rest of the orthodox Jewish community, we have always had a degree of objectivity. Now is a time to put that objectivity, and its consequent clarity of vision, to good purpose, and to show the rest of the community the way: leaving the Union may be only a small gesture, and it may only be a start, but it is at least a start to putting our community back on the sound moral basis which is its only justification for existing in the first place.

41

Time for Action – Kosher Meat and Kosher Behaviour

I am delighted to record that Nissims the butchers is still in business, 7 years on from when I wrote this piece. But another new butcher is just about to open up within yards of their shop, and those of the Jewish community who have enough of a conscience to connect religion and decency will have to step up our efforts again. (From 5th February 2010)

There is a lovely family kosher butcher's shop on Brent Street called Nissim. They are fine upstanding people, who serve good quality food at reasonable prices, and whose behaviour is as kosher as the meat that they serve.

And they are likely to be put out of business any month now.

A chain of kosher butchers who already have branches in Golders Green and elsewhere are about to open up a new shop within a few yards of Nissims. They have economy of scale advantages, and will doubtless dent or destroy the Nissims' business.

The Rabbis should prevent this, and could. The Biblical precept of not disturbing your neighbours' boundaries is given extensive ramifications in Jewish business ethics, and no Beth Din ought to grant a licence to a shop that is about to destroy someone else's business, unless it is clearly shown that the existing business is exploiting its monopoly.

But the Rabbis won't act. Years ago, a Rabbinic representative of the London Beth Din told me that they do not consider it practicable to apply or enforce the din of hasogas gvul (your neighbour's borders), primarily because they are not the only Beth Din in London. So people can always get licensed somewhere else.

If the Rabbis are in disarray and unable to give practical expression to the values of the Torah, we must take matters into our own hands. Let us see a customer boycott of any shop opening within a few yards of an existing business, and let's all shop at Nissims harder than ever.

42

Sense and Sensibility – The Bournemouth Lights Fiasco

"Religious person shows a modicum of sense" is a head-line that is unlikely to sell newspapers; "daft twit behaves stupidly in the name of religion" is a more promising read ... (From 16th June 2009)

The BBC news is reporting today that a couple are suing the management company of their Bournemouth flat for installing automatic light sensors that will prevent them from using their flat on shabbos. They are claiming religious discrimination.

Just a few thoughts.

First and foremost, this raises general issues about the use of laws on religious and other discrimination. Laws are no substitute for sense and sensitivity – not to mention manners – all round. The fact that laws have to be cast in wide terms does not mean it is always appropriate to rely upon them: to insist upon one's rights can sometimes help to turn us into a selfish and litigious society, rather than a caring and sensitive one.

Secondly, who have these people asked about the position on shabbos? I do not know the precise circumstances of their flat and the positioning and use of these lights. But based on the facts in the news report, if it is forbidden by halochoh to walk past these sensors and turn the lights on, then I am a baked hedgehog with mushroom sauce. Yes, the lights will certainly come on each time – but that doesn't make it forbidden to walk past them: for those interested in the technicalities, it is a din of misaseik rather than a din of psik reisho[13]. Of course, every case is different and what is permitted in one context may be forbidden in another – but on an issue like this one would need to consult one of the gedolei hador (which for all I know they may have done). A little halachic knowledge is always worse than none – and can lead one to go seriously wrong in either direction.

Thirdly, what sort of impression will this give their neighbours of the way Jews behave? Answer: if they lose, bad – and if they win, worse. Why should I insist that my religious principles should cause other people to spend extra money on equipment and electricity, contrary to their economic interests and ecological principles? Not burdening one's neighbours is a significant halachic principle. Standing on our rights rarely makes people think well of us.

I may be misjudging these people and their situation seriously – because my comments are based only on the BBC news report: but from what I can make of that, it is possible the whole episode is a serious misjudgement, neither required nor desirable in accordance with

---

[13] Misaseik – something superimposed externally on my permitted action; psik reisho – inevitable prohibited by-product of my permitted action.

halochoh. Of course, there are other factors one would need to take into account before forming a judgment about this behaviour: in particular, what contractual or other commitments were given on the acquisition of the lease and by whom; and what attempts have been made to resolve this issue without recourse to the courts. Overall, the news report makes uncomfortable reading, and reminds us of the importance of doing whatever we can to treat, and be seen to treat, our host countries in exile with respect and gratitude, and not to appear to be overly demanding or insensitive to other people's rights and values.

43

The London Eruv

Just when we thought London orthodox Jewry had enough divisions in its ranks to satisfy even the most pugnacious and quarrelsome, along came the Eruv ... (From 22nd March 2008)

For the last few years I have relied on the London Eruv without any qualms. As my Rav whom I first consulted about the matter remarked, "Dayan Ehrentreu is a reasonably orthodox gentleman ...".

This week I received, unsolicited, a glossy booklet called "The Eruv HaMehudar in NW London" published by Friends of the North-West London Eruv. Everything about it suggests spin worthy of a dodgy double-glazing firm. The result of its pages of selective quotations, questionable translations and effusive peroration is that for the first time ever I am seriously doubtful about the kashrus of the eruv. If it needs this kind of advertising propaganda, I seriously wonder whether there is not something wrong with it.

Before receiving this booklet, it would never have occurred to me to try to assess the issues surrounding the eruv: that is a matter for rabbonim mumchim b'hilchos eruv,[14] not for me. But this booklet purports to explain the reasons for the eruv's kashrus b'hiddur and in effect invites me to consider them. So I have read it, and contrasted it with the commendably measured responses published in this week's Jewish Tribune (a publication which I bought for the first time in many years for this purpose) from the Union of Orthodox Hebrew Congregations and a world-renowned Rov whose letter is printed in the booklet.

My conclusion is that this is clearly an eruv: but to call it mehudar,[15] and to suggest that it is endorsed by the gedolei Torah generally, is seriously misleading: the kashrus of the eruv depends in essence on reliance on a single minority opinion of the Chazon Ish.

So those who rely on the eruv have something on which to rely, as well as Dayonim on whom to rely; and those who regard it as insufficient also have much on which to rely. I am now clear, which I was not before, that this is not a question of divisive politics on behalf of those who reject the kashrus of the eruv: they have strong grounds for believing that carrying within the eruv is genuine chillul shabbos.

In other words, we are in territory of eilu v'eilu divrei elokim chayim.[16] Many who wish to be machmir in their shabbos observance will choose not to rely on the eruv; those who have particular family or other reasons to wish to rely on an eruv will probably continue to do so. The important thing is to ensure that both groups treat each other with sensitivity, understanding, respect and love.

---

[14] Rabbis expert in the laws of the eruv boundary.
[15] Compliant with the most exacting standards.
[16] A rabbinic dictum – "both the words of these and the words of these are the words of the living God".

44

The who is a Jew Crisis – whose fault?

The JFS "Who is a Jew?" case exposed internal workings of the Jewish community as perhaps never before. It has all died down, with a solution that has led to a bit of a muddle and a number of anomalies (including Christian families turning up regularly to Shabbos services in synagogue in order to acquire enough attendance points to secure entrance for their children into sought-after state funded schools). It might have been an opportunity to take an objective look at ourselves and tighten up certain communal institutions; but we didn't ... (From 16th March 2008)

The British Jewish community is now in serious trouble, its right to have schools for Jews threatened on two sides. The High Court is about to decide whether JFS can apply its admissions criteria by reference to exclusively orthodox criteria of Jewish status. And the government has recently changed, and is currently in the process of a critical examination of the application of, the laws of selective admission as they relate to faith schools.

The surest way to resolve both crises is to determine whose fault they are.

In typical style, the British Jewish community has already offered a number of possible public answers to that: The Chief Rabbi, the London Beth Din, the parents of the children challenging admissions.

In other words, everyone except the rank and file of the British Jewish community: but it is we who have brought this on ourselves.

A reform leader went on the BBC Radio 4 this morning to explain that the JFS crisis is because ortho-dox rabbis do not recognise "all" decisions of the reform, so that "technically" the child is not Jewish.

An orthodox rabbi was asked to reply to that – so he said, "Judaism is not a democracy – you have to abide by the rules."

Which is the point. When judges or Ministers examine our community to see these selective rules in application, they will see that we enforce them strictly only against people on the outside looking in. Once a person is accepted as "technically" Jewish, they can eat what they like, do what they like, and nobody regards them as beyond the pale of the community. But the product of a reform conversion, who may observe more of the rules of kashrut than 90% of our community, who may pray to God more often than 95% of our community, is dismissed as unworthy to mix with our children because of being not Jewish.

This attitude is halachically sound, but spiritually bankrupt. While we as a community hold our own rules of religion in apparent contempt, why should we expect judges or Ministers to accord respect to any of them?

In the tochahah warnings, God warns that if we behave as if the world is without a ruler, He will allow the world to carry on as if it were. Here too, if we behave as though being Jewish is a matter of mere genetics, God will show us the emptiness and futility of that approach.

So the only real answer is, as always, nachp'so derocheinu venoshuvo – to sort out our own communal behaviour. If we can live in a way which gives the impression that the rules of the Torah and the rabbis are worthy of respect, perhaps others outside the community will be encouraged to follow suit.

45

Women-Only Concerts and Sex Discrimination

Sometimes secularism and religion will simply collide no matter how much one tries to pretend that tolerance on both sides will inevitably lead to peaceful coexistence. For example, in the secular world equality between the sexes is by now a non-negotiable; and yet in orthodox Judaism it has limits that are distinctly challenging in the modern world. (From 10th July 2005)

Next Sunday evening the Logan Hall in London will host a concert by girls and women (including my daughter Shira) for girls and women. No men will be admitted, in order to comply with the halacha which prohibits men from listening to women singing (and therefore prohibits women from singing to men).

This concert may or may not be lawful as a matter of the law of England and Wales. Section 29(2)(e) of the Sex Discrimination Act 1975 (taken with sections 2 and 4(3)) makes it unlawful to refuse to provide to men facilities for entertainment that are being provided to women. A possible saving for the legality of the concert is the exception in section 35(1)(b): but the application of that exception depends on what is meant by "the place is (permanently or for the time being) occupied or used for the purposes of an organised religion". The meaning of that phrase is debatable (I did not write it – but I have had to consider it in drafting the Equality Bill that is presently before Parliament). And there are other exceptions which may, or may not, apply.

So much for the narrow point of discrimination law in relation to next week's concert. In practice it is of no importance: in the circumstances it is inconceivable that anyone would wish to bring a challenge under the 1975 Act to the staging of this concert for an all-female audience.

There is, however, an underlying question of greater potential importance. Considerable attention has been given to the strengthening of anti-discrimination law as an additional protection for religion, both in Part 2 of the Equality Bill mentioned above (and in the proposed new law about the incitement of religious hatred). But possibly of greater significance for religious communities is the extent to which other strengthenings of anti-discrimination law could conflict with religious practice and belief.

Sex-discrimination is relevant here, and apart from single-sex concerts it is not difficult to think of instances of segregation in the Jewish religious community that are arguably already unlawful as a matter of secular law, although for the present (but who knows for how long) it is unlikely that anyone would seek to enforce the law in these respects.

But other forms of discrimination may be even more problematic. Newly strengthened protection against discrimination on grounds of sexual orientation has the potential to be a particular problem. In the employment context, for example, I have always believed that it would be unnecessary and improper for a Jewish school to refuse to employ, say, a music teacher merely because there was reason to believe that he might be homosexual. But I have always believed equally strongly that it would be absolutely necessary to refuse to employ a teacher who thought it right actively to publicise in school, whether by wearing a badge or in any other way, the fact that he indulged in homosexual practices (in the same way that it would be absolutely necessary to refuse to employ a teacher who was openly indulging in an adulterous relationship). Homosexual practice (as distinct from a feeling or affiliation) and adultery are two straightforward prohibitions of the Torah; and to suggest to our school-children that these prohibitions are to be tolerated to the extent of not rendering a person unfit to be a teacher would be incompatible with the fundamental purpose of a Jewish school.

It needs to be recognised, however, that a refusal of employment in these circumstances might already be contrary to civil law; and this may be just one of an increasing range of potential sources of tension between traditional Jewish belief and practice and the modern secular British ethos.

The courts have already had occasion to observe that when the dictates of religious or other tradition conflict with the fundamental principles of freedom, tolerance and self-determination on which secular British society is based, it is the latter that must prevail. See, for example, the observations of Mr Justice Singer in *Re KR (a child) (abduction: forcible removal by parents)* [1999] 4 All

ER 954. And there is much still to be explored about the possibility of fundamental incompatibility between the European Convention on Human Rights' protection for freedom of religion and its other protections.

So we should be aware that the general religious tolerance in Britain – which represents much of what attracted many of our ancestors to this country and for which we are all deeply grateful – does not mean that our religious values may not sometimes create direct conflict with the secular law and values on which that tolerance is based.

JEWISH THOUGHT

46

The Binding of Isaac –
Who's Testing Whom?

In inter-faith dialogue, much is made of the idea that the three Abrahamic religions are bound together by ties of shared ancestry and, therefore, shared values. As someone who was prepared to risk murdering his son on the grounds of what he believed to be a divine command communicated to himself in a vision, at first sight Abraham might not be the most sound or reliable personality on which to base even one person's confidence, far less the shared values of a large part of the theoretically civilised world. As someone who was, however, prepared to challenge God in no uncertain terms, so as to question the consistency of God's message, Abraham makes a more reliable foundation for a religious personality. In forging an alliance between the major religions of today, more emphasis needs to be placed on Abraham's willingness to challenge religious dictate when it appeared contrary to instinctive values of decency, and less emphasis on his commitment to monotheism per se. One God is just as dangerous as many gods; and arguably more dangerous, if he is thought to be telling his followers to do daft things... (From 27th September 2014)

We read the story of the binding of Isaac yesterday as we do every year at New Year.

For years this story bothered me: what sort of a person is prepared to sacrifice his or her son to God, and what kind of God demands that sacrifice?

The Torah singles out the idolatry of Molech as particularly objectionable on precisely the grounds of child sacrifice.

So this may have been the tenth test of Abraham by God: but what was the point? To find out if Abraham was prepared to be barbaric?

I finally realised this year that the anxiety underpinning my issues with this story was simply "What if it had gone wrong?"

Of course, the Midrash says that Isaac's neck was turned to marble so that when Abraham tried to show his real determination to do whatever God demanded of him, he couldn't harm his son.

So Abraham was prepared to be barbaric and God had to stop him? Again, what kind of a person does that make Abraham?

I have finally found an answer that sort of satisfies me, at least for the moment.

If Isaac had died, Abraham would have stopped believing in God.

This was about Abraham testing God. As he said at Sodom – "cholilo lecho ..." – it is unthinkable for the God I know to punish the innocent for the sins of the wicked. Here he is saying to God, if you make me kill my son to show my love for you, I will know that you are not worth loving.

Many rabbis have said over the years that Abraham did not expect to be asked to kill Isaac in the end. It would have contradicted Abraham's entire conception of God as a God of justice and mercy. But until he put the knife to Isaac's throat in response to the Divine command, Abraham may have believed that Isaac would not have been allowed to die: but he could not have known it with certainty.

The end of the test showed Abraham with absolute certainty that his earlier assessment of God's ideals was correct, and that the values of justice, compassion and peace are indeed the foundations of our belief in and commitment to God.

So, as someone asked me at the table yesterday: why is this presented as a test of Abraham, not a test of God.

The answer is: the final test of Abraham was whether he was prepared to test God: was he prepared to set limits to his commitment to God, parameters to his belief, which he could not cross while remaining devoted to God's service?

We read this story on Rosh Hashanah as we set out to forge a new relationship with God at the start of the new year: to remind us that our relationship must be based on underpinning values, which bound and explain our conception of God.

A person who will obey any command that comes from a religious book, a religious leader or even a religious vision, and never question or challenge it, is not a believer: he or she is an obsessive fanatic with no ideals or values underneath blind faith.

As Jews, our faith is not in God, but in the characteristics that He has taught us as Divine: the thirteen attributes of God are in the fact the parameters of our belief.

When our religion tallies with the human instincts that are part of the Divine image in which we are created, we know we are on the right track.

Hopefully this will be a year in which religious people around the world will listen increasingly to the promptings of our sound human instincts, so that religion can become a force that unites us in getting the best out of our common humanity.

47

Miracle-workers and Money

So long as there are people who are ready to believe in God, there will be other people ready to exploit that belief for their own personal gain. The bogus miracle worker is not unique to Judaism, and indeed mainstream Judaism has been perhaps relatively untroubled by this practice. Some may say that if people are stupid enough to fall for this kind of nonsense then that is their own look out. Others would say that communities need to look after the vulnerable within them, and that includes people whose degree of desperation or longing has made them particularly susceptible to exploitation by crooks of the kind described below. (From 18th September 2011)

The latest copy of the free *London Jewish Advertiser* – a useful advertising magazine which I have always liked and admired because it has never pretended to carry any kind of substance other than advertising – contains an advertisement that one can only hope is simply a cruel and tasteless fraud.

The text of this full-page advertisement says as follows: "A G-d fearing man of great ability who lives in Israel, can heal people of cancer from one day to the next. He asks with every lashon of bakashah that women DO NOT contact him but a man should contact him or her behalf. Please speak only in Hebrew as the man doesn't understand English at all. There are 2 things that need to be prepared: 1. To prepare a CT scan where there is a cancerous growth. 2. To phone the man above to arrange a mutual third party who you will agree to deposit an agreed amount of money, either at a Beis Din, Rav, lawyer etc., and to pay the agreed deposit to the third party. The man will then prepare a tikun and then to get a new CT scan from the hospital. If the illness has gone within 1 WEEK, then he will take the money as agreed from the third party. IF, HOWEVER, the illness has not gone then the man will not take any money at all!"

Hopefully, this is just a plain and simple fraud, in which case presumably someone will by now have arranged for the police in Israel to do the necessary.

But what was the *Advertiser* thinking of printing this stuff? The *Advertiser* is circulated to houses with mezuzot in orthodox Jewish areas, and is aimed at the orthodox Jewish community. Presumably, if someone wanted to insert an advert for pornography, the advertisement would be refused. Is there nobody capable of exercising enough editorial discretion to work out that this advertisement is either (a) a simple fraud, or (b) at the very least, every bit as tasteless as an advert for pornography?

Either this man has special powers or he doesn't. If he doesn't, the advertisement is a crude attempt to extort money from the vulnerable. If he does, the advertisement is a crude assertion that these powers are to be made available only in return for payment, which is contrary to every notion of orthodox Judaism as I understand it.

What troubles me is that this is by far the first – although certainly the crudest and most tasteless – emergence of attempts to exploit religious credulity within the orthodox community. The number of glossy brochures for orthodox charities which now openly promise "yeshuos" – salvations – and publicise past miracles received by donors, seems to increase all the time. And several miracle workers – blatantly advertised as such – have been brought to the country and publicised in straightforward marketing exercises.

So it is time for the Jewish community to reassert that we are a community united by religion, not by superstition, and that we are not all entirely stupid.

The power of prayer and blessing is an intense and real part of the Jewish religion – but it has never meant miracles to order, and those whose prayers and blessings are genuine, and therefore will sometimes be efficacious, bestow them in a selfless and altruistic manner, without thought of payment whether on a conditional basis as suggested by this advertisement or otherwise.

An advertisement proclaiming powers to control divine intervention and offering to exercise them in return for payment is such a shameless parody of the concepts of blessing and prayer that the editors of the Advertiser should have seen from a mile off that to include it in their magazine would have been to subject their readers to gross offense.

Hopefully the next issue will carry an unequivocal apology.

48

Messiah Delayed – Moschiach Can't Get Through

The thought about the incongruity of bad manners and religious observance expressed at the beginning of the last piece rattled around in my head and became, and remains, something of an obsession. In an attempt to exorcise it to some extent, I turned it into a kind of pastiche upon a well-known rabbinic prophecy concerning the arrival of the Messiah. (From 29th April 2011)

When the Rabbis wrote, basing themselves on the verse in Psalms 95 "… today if you would listen to his voice", that the Messiah sets out every day to travel on his donkey to the Western Wall they were, of course, speaking allegorically. Nowadays he goes by bus.

He starts every day at the bus-stop just outside one of the non-religious kibbutzim in the North of Israel. He waits patiently among a crowd of Israeli youths who stand around talking and joking with each other. Many of them are smoking, none of them is dressed particularly modestly, and the nature of their language is not always of the cleanest. "But, after all", thinks

Moschiach, "they don't know any better – they come from a non-religious culture, and if they're no better than any other group of humans at least they're no worse." He struggles onto the bus trying not to feel too disheartened, and stands because the seats are all taken: then one of the girls notices an elderly man or woman standing and abruptly motions one of her companions to make way. Moschiach sits down feeling slightly reassured.

Moschiach changes buses at the central bus station in Tel Aviv. He waits among a crowd of businessmen and businesswomen on their way to Jerusalem for mid-morning meetings; some men wearing kippot and some not, some married women covering their hair and others not. They ignore each other and jabber into their mobiles or poke away at little keyboards. When the bus comes they all shove on treating each other with entirely passive hostility. "But, after all," thinks Moschiach, "they're busy, thinking about making money to look after their families, and if they're no better than any other group of humans at least they're no worse." Then one of the businesswomen happens to glance up and see an elderly woman or man standing, and abruptly motions a businessman she's never met to make way. Moschiach sits down feeling distinctly hopeful.

Moschiach changes buses again at the central bus station in Jerusalem. He waits among a crowd of soldiers going to the Old City. They stand around smoking and talking morosely. When the bus comes they use their kitbags as battering rams to make their way through the crowds and fling themselves down in the seats, eyeing the other passengers struggling on after them with disinterest or mild animosity. "But, after all," thinks Moschiach, "they're nervous and preoccupied, and they're little more than children with adult responsibilities thrust on them, and if they're no better than any other crowd of soldiers at least they're no worse." Then one of them sees an elderly man or woman crushed against the mountain of kit-bags and without much grace gets up and motions at his seat. Moschiach sits down feeling rather excited.

The final change of bus is in Meah Shearim, just outside the Toldos Aharon courtyard. Moschiach looks around: the placards on the wall proclaim that only the modestly dressed may walk through this holy neighbourhood; everywhere the signs of Torah learning and Torah observance meet the eye; shops piled high with holy books, men and boys on their way to or from learning sessions talking animatedly of their studies, women shepherding their young families along the narrow pavements; walls placarded with pronouncements of the great rabbis of the generation; the air buzzes with the "chareidi" Torah atmosphere. Moschiach is elated.

Then the bus comes. The crowd of chareidim charge at it without a thought for who came before or after whom. Men push women aside with unthinking violence. The elderly are shoved away unless they show an aggression that ill befits their years. Children are separated from their parents and dragged or pushed back impatiently. The rabbi who was preaching kindness and the unity of the Jewish nation just a few minutes ago is squeezing himself into the front of the queue although he only just got there. Moschiach sighs, and turns away. As the bus pulls out the rabbi thinks he saw an elderly woman standing on the pavement: he looks back, but he was mistaken – there is nobody there.

49

Did Sarah Suffer from Senile Dementia?

As people live longer, senile dementia and other mental diseases associated with age become more common, and therefore more and more of us are frightened of succumbing to them in later life. Dementia appears to be remarkably impartial in its choices of victims, and neither extreme intelligence nor extreme stupidity appear to be guarantees against falling victim to it. Musing about it one day made me start to wonder about rabbinic accounts of the death of Sarah. (Incidentally, the elderly gentleman referred to in this piece was Rabbi Cooper, whom I discuss also in Chapter 30: as with that appreciation of his life, members of his family contacted me after the publication of this piece saying that they had recognised the allusion and that they approved of its message.) (From 14th January 2009)

The Rabbis tell us that the Matriarch Sarah – Soroh Imeinu – died the "kiss-like" death reserved for the completely righteous, where they slip almost imperceptibly from one world into the next.

But what was she like before her death? Did she go to sleep one night in possession of all her faculties and pass tranquilly to the next world in her sleep? Or did the transition take place over a longer period, and was it accompanied by a gradual loss of the intellectual faculties that tie us to this world as much as the more tangible part of the corporeal side of our personality? Did she gradually slip more and more "into her own world", with less and less ability to connect with and understand this one, until she finally slipped altogether into the next?

Doctors tell us that dementia is becoming more common. This may be a function of the increased stress under which we live. Or it may reflect the improved ability of medical science to keep our bodies going longer. Probably it is a combination of many factors. But whatever its cause, it is a condition with which more and more people come to terms.

In an old-age home somewhere in London lives a man, whose age would once have been thought advanced but is now nothing remarkable. Ten years ago, he was renowned for his piety and his intellect. His learning was considered by those entitled to an opinion to rank him as one of the foremost Talmudic and rabbinic scholars in the world.

Now he sits in his old age home, often unsure what is going on around him, unable to remember many things that one needs to remember in order to function effectively in this world and to look after oneself. And I sometimes hear people mention him and add something like "isn't it a shame, when one thinks what he was?"

Depending on precisely what they mean, they are either right or terribly wrong. When a wise and active scholar ceases to be able to use his or her brain in the way they once could, it is indeed a shame – but for us, not for them. We lose the benefit of their wisdom and intellect, which was once such an important Divine blessing for us. We would have lost it, of course, had they simply died: but it is more frustrating for us this way, seeing their faculties wane gradually, and seeing them alive and well physically but no longer able to give us the help and guidance that we so desperately need and at which they once excelled. And if it is frustrating for us, how terrible must it be for those close to them emotionally – their relatives and close friends.

Of course, though, we must try to control our grief in the same way we do when a person simply dies. The Rabbis explain the small letter used in the word describing Abraham's grief when Sarah died by the fact that not too many tears were needed to be shed for her, since her life had been such an unalloyed blessing to her and those around her, so that joy and not grief was the more durable emotion to be associated with her forever. That is true of a person whose contribution has been great, whether it is brought to an end suddenly by death or gradually by disease.

And if by "what a shame!" is meant "what a shame for them", it misses the point completely. The man I speak of was once a great soul and a great mind. His mind is no longer great, but his soul shines out all the more brightly for that. We are not normally privileged to see the purity of a soul while it is still bound to this world: on rare occasions we are privileged to see what decades' dedicated practice of the Torah can make of a person's moral and spiritual instincts – so that long after they are able to control much of their behaviour by the intellect the ingrained characteristics of love, gratitude and concern (all Divine attributes) shine out of them and make them a source of wonder and inspiration to all who see them.

We too easily mistake the mind for the soul. A person may be a brilliant intellect, a charismatic, dynamic speaker, a charming personality, and spiritually inert. Brilliant Talmudic dialectic is a thing of this world, not the next: it can be used to guard and develop a person's soul so that when the intellect fails the soul shines out in all its original purity – but in itself it is spiritually neutral.

Of course, dementia brings moments of mental pain, anguish and confusion; just like other physical diseases. And when we see them we feel a sympathetic distress. But, again, that may sometimes be our problem, not the person's. If a friend who once knew me well no longer recognises me, that upsets me – but I must not make the mistake of thinking that it necessarily upsets him or her; or that it is their problem rather than mine.

Thinking of the increasing incidence of dementia makes me want to pray.

Not—

"Dear God, please don't let me suffer from dementia before I die".

But rather something a little more confused along the following lines—

"Dear God, please help me to use the mental faculties I have while I can still control them, so that when I stop being able to control them, whether that happens before I die or when I die, they have done their bit to make the real me – the soul and not the brain – something that you and I can rejoice in; and, please, if I am to go through a period of inability to control my mind before I die, help me to use it in the meantime to put the "real me", whatever that is, into sufficient shape to ensure that those who are close to me do not have to suffer the pain of being ashamed of me".

50

Sight and Sound – how we see and hear the world

Mass hypnosis is quite a tempting explanation for supposed religious revelations. Based on rabbinic discussions of the Biblical account of the revelation of Judaism, it may not be so far from the truth. Of course, like most scientific explanations, it begs the questions of who or what induced the phenomenon, and why... (From 26th January 2008)

In this morning's Torah reading, Yisro hears and reacts (Shemos 18:1). He hears world news available to everybody else – news about the Jews' exit from Egypt – but he has a greater than normal capacity to understand the implications, and to allow them to cause him to change his entire mode of life and to become a monotheist.

Later in the reading we have a physical impossibility – the Jews at Mount Sinai see voices (Shemos 20:19). That could indicate an entirely transcendental experience; or it could suggest merely a heightened perception, an enhancement of the natural sense of vision to a degree at which it was capable of perceiving the sounds.

We can prove which it was from Rashi: he comments (from the Mechilta) that "all the nation saw" shows that no blind people were at Sinai. If by seeing sounds we were referring to something wholly unnatural, why should blind people be less able to do it than sighted people? So it must have been a natural use of sight, but enhanced to an unusual degree of refinement.

Both these are the essence of the Jewish approach to the world. We do not claim to be able to hear or see things that other people cannot. But we believe that concentration on spiritual values can lead human beings to be able to understand more of what they hear, and to see aspects of happenings that other might miss. The world is full of blessings and miracles, but we need to train ourselves to notice them and to understand their implications.

This also explains something about the nature of ruach hakodesh.[17] Some people have trained their spiritual sensitivities, by close adherence to Torah values, so that they understand more than I do of what God wants from the world and is doing to the world. By consulting them I may not learn things that I did not already know, but I may come to understand them better or to see aspects of them that were hidden to me. Similarly, when chassidim seek a brochoh from a Rebbe they are asking him to apply his more refined understanding of the world to confirm whether they are moving in paths that make proper use of their blessings and that reflect understanding of events around them.

---

[17] Divine spirit.

51

Humour in Jewish thought

I am increasingly suspicious of people and groups who cannot laugh at themselves. Humour in general – but self-directed humour in particular – is an important safeguard of sanity. Taking oneself too seriously is both a sign of a troubled mind and a reliable precursor to a vicious cycle of more trouble. Judaism and humour have always gone together. And the increasingly serious-minded groups of orthodox Jews for whom humour is somehow suspect and indicative of an insufficiently serious and spiritual mind, are easy to recognise as a dangerous perversion of Judaism simply by their inability to laugh at themselves. But as for everything, there is a time and a place ... (From 9th April 2006)

The recent incident in which a comedian performing at a Jewish charity event gave offence by a particularly tasteless routine prompts me to offer a few thoughts about the Torah's attitude towards humour in general.

Maimonides declares that laughter or merriment (s'chok) will have no place in the world to come (Hilchos Teshuvah 8:2). But its inhabitants will feel a contentment described by some of the prophets as happiness (simchah).

And yet there is no general sense in Jewish thought that laughter is in itself evil. Indeed, in a number of places in aggadic literature God is metaphorically depicted as laughing. Koheles, typically, reveals the ambivalence of the Torah towards humour. In one place laughter (s'chok) and even pleasure (simchah) are completely dismissed as futile (2:2). Later it is asserted that there is a time for laughter (3:4). And later still great emphasis is put on the positive effects of joy – 8:passim).

There are thousands of Biblical and rabbinic statements regarding different kinds of emotion to which humour may contribute or be relevant, and it would be more than a lifetime's work to construct a completely balanced view of the Torah's attitude to these. What is clear is that humour, levity and light-heartedness have an approved place, but they are also associated with a number of dangers (some kinds in particular – most notably flippancy or scoffing (leitzonus)).

The best overview that I have ever found of the various distinctions comes from a Christian theologian, C S Lewis. In *The Screwtape Letters* he writes a series of letters of instruction purporting to come from a senior devil to a relative novice, instructing him in how to lead human beings away from the paths of virtue. His passage on joy and humour is so powerful and brilliant an exposition of what I believe to be the Torah attitude on the subject that I think it worth quoting here at considerable length (although not quite in full).

"I divide the causes of human laughter into Joy, Fun, the Joke Proper, and Flippancy. You will see the first among friends and lovers reunited on the eve of a holiday. Among adults some pretext in the way of Jokes is usually provided, but the facility with which the smallest witticisms produce laughter at such a time shows that they are not the real cause. What the real cause is we do not know. Something like it is expressed in much of that detestable art which the humans call Music, and something like it occurs in Heaven – a meaningless acceleration in the rhythm of celestial experience, quite opaque to us. Laughter of this kind does us no good and should always be discouraged. ...

"Fun is closely related to Joy – a sort of emotional froth arising from the play instinct. It is of very little use to us. It can sometimes be used, of course, to divert humans from something else which [God] would like them to be feeling or doing: but in itself it has wholly undesirable tendencies; it promotes charity, courage, contentment, and many other evils.

"The Joke Proper, which turns on sudden perception of incongruity, is a much more promising field. ... The real use of Jokes or Humour is in quite a different direction, and it is specially promising among the English who take their 'sense of humour' so seriously that a deficiency in this sense is almost the only deficiency at which they feel shame. Humour is for them the all-consoling and (mark this) the all-excusing, grace of life. Hence it is invaluable as a means of destroying shame.

If a man simply lets others pay for him, he is 'mean'; if he boasts of it in a jocular manner and twits his fellows with having been scored off, he is no longer 'mean' but a comical fellow. Mere cowardice is shameful; cowardice boasted of with humorous exaggerations and grotesque gestures can be passed off as funny. Cruelty is shameful – unless the cruel man can represent it as a practical joke. A thousand bawdy, or even blasphemous, jokes do not help towards a man's damnation so much as his discovery that almost anything he wants to do can be done, not only without the disapproval but with the admiration of his fellows, if only it can get itself treated as a Joke. ...

"But Flippancy is best of all. ... If prolonged, the habit of Flippancy builds up around a man the finest armour-plating against [God] that I know, and it is quite free from the dangers inherent in the other sources of laughter. It is a thousand miles away from joy: it deadens, instead of sharpening, the intellect; and it excites no affection between those who practice it."

52

Rabbinic Infallibility

The tendency to assign unblemished saintliness to Biblical characters and the early rabbis, and to invest contemporary rabbis with a kind of papal infallibility, is a modern and troubling distortion of Judaism. Rabbis often get things wrong, and only a fool would think that they wouldn't. The concept of trust in the sages is a key precept of orthodox Judaism, but it has traditionally been very far away from anything like a belief in their infallibility. Although blind trust in anyone else as a moral guide inevitably leads to disappointment and trouble, it is become increasingly common, presumably because if I rely on a rabbi to set spiritual standards for me I am relieved from the painful necessity of thinking for myself. (From 4th March 2006)

The post *Passive Smoking* (Chapter 74), attracted some interesting questions and comments by email, including one asking whether the fact that the Pnei Yehoshuah thought that smoking was good for you suggests something about rabbinic infallibility, or rather the lack of it.

The position in Torah thought about the status of rabbinic pronouncements is clear in principle, although not always easy to apply in practice. The essence of the approach is to determine which of many possible functions a particular rabbi is performing when he speaks or writes.

At one extreme, the rabbis may expound the meaning of the written Torah or the latest developments of the oral Torah (in accordance with the exegetical principles given to Moshe Rabbeinu on Har Sinai) or enact decrees to reflect the needs of their time. We have an express biblical obligation to observe the Torah in accordance with the rabbis' pronouncements and decrees which are therefore, if not exactly infallible, certainly beyond challenge (whether by reference to objective accuracy or to any other matter).

So, for example, the Talmud records that when the rabbis made an objective error in calculating the dates of Yom Tov and the angels objected to God, He told them not to interfere (and there are other similar Talmudic passages). Similarly, until the Cohen pronounces that a house is affected by tzora'as,[18] it is not affected and vessels may be removed from it, but once the pronouncement is made any remaining vessels become affected: illogical, given that the nature of the tzora'as has not changed during the process, but explicable by reference to the power that the Torah gives to the pronouncements and decisions of the rabbis (originally, the Cohanim).

At the other extreme, the rabbis sometimes speak or write merely to record or transmit information. If the

---

[18] Sometimes mis-translated as leprosy – a divine visitation that attracts certain laws of tum'o (which is sometimes mis-translated as impurity).

information is wrong, either because the rabbi in question was supplied with deficient data or because his techniques of observation or calculation were limited or faulty, there is nothing heretical about disregarding the information when its deficiencies become apparent. So, for example, early parts of the Mishneh Torah record certain astronomical information which has been shown by later techniques of observation to be erroneous: the Rambam thought it would be helpful to record the latest scientific understanding of these matters in the Mishneh Torah, but that does not give them any kind of Torah authority or infallibility.

Between these two extremes is an important grey area. In particular, where the rabbis give halachic decisions which are expressly based on stated information, the decision will be open to challenge if it is shown that the information is flawed.

(See, in this connection, Rav Moshe Feinstein's introduction to the Igros Moshe, where he explains why he gives his reasoning in full in each decision.)

In the case mentioned in the last issue, the Pnei Yehoshuah gave a decision about smoking on Yom Tov expressly based on the best medical evidence available to him at the time as to the beneficial effects on the digestive system of smoking. Now that the medical evidence has changed, there is nothing heretical in disregarding the Pnei Yehoshuah's psak halochoh and asking the rabbis of today to start again to determine the halochoh based on the present state of medical evidence; indeed, any other approach would be to ascribe to factual statements of the rabbis an infallibility and authority that could itself be seen as heretical.

53

Pinchos and terrorism

It is an uncomfortable reality that political and religious violence has been part of Jewish history both ancient and modern. Biblical stories of violence shouldn't be simply ignored, but confronted and placed into context. And we should not be ashamed of the possibility that despite the Jewish idea that understanding of the Torah diminishes as we get further from Mount Sinai, ethical sensitivity may be becoming more refined in a number of ways over the years. (From 21ˢᵗ July 2005)

A religious zealot who in his determination to rid the world of the wickedness and idolatry of the unbeliever bypasses the rule of law and the judicial processes (even those established by his own religion) and takes it upon himself to impose and carry out a summary death sentence on wrongdoers as a public act of vengeance, following which his god grants him, according to his religion, a reward of a covenant of peace and eternal life.

A chilling description of the behaviour of certain terrorists acting in the name of Islam today.

But is it also an accurate description of the behaviour of Pinchos in last week's parashah and his reward in this?

Pinchos is a zealot, for which characteristic he is expressly commended and rewarded (Bamidbar 25:11). He acts when the established leaders of the Jewish people consider themselves, deeply regretfully, unable to act in accordance with Torah law to suppress acknowledged idolatrous wrong-doing (25:6-7). He imposes and carries out a summary death penalty (25:8). The reward for his violence is a special hereditary bond with God and a promise of peace (Bamidbar 25:12-13).

There are of course a multitude of differences between Pinchos' behaviour and the behaviour of today's terrorists acting in the name of Islam. The most significant is that Pinchos confined his anger to those who were directly responsible for performing idolatry in a deliberately provocative, offensive and public manner: the modern terrorists target the innocent along with the guilty. And he acted only because he knew these wrong-doers to have incurred liability in accordance with Torah law for the death penalty, and that Moses and the elders were incapacitated as a result of righteous self-doubt born of Zimri's sharp accusations about a superficial similarity of Moses' own marital circumstances with the contemporary idolatrous behaviour. Finally, Pinchos was able to trust that his violence on this occasion was motivated only by a proper desire to preserve the dignity of God because he had trained his instincts so that his normal inclinations were to be a true exponent of the love of peace exemplified by his grandfather Aharon.

But a striking aspect of every one of the differences specified above is that in each case Pinchos' righteousness is not apparent on the face of the Torah but depends on a knowledge of the midrashic and rabbinic constructions of the circumstances of his activities.

There is another striking example in this week's parashah of a similar notion. God tells Moses to attack the Midianites (25:17 and 31:2). But Moses does not perform this commandment himself, but appoints Pinchos as leader of the army (31:6). The rabbis explain that Moses thought it would be wrong for him to attack the Midianites personally because they had sheltered him on his escape from Egypt (Shemos 2:15). But since when was it for Moses to alter God's commandment because he thought it wrong?! I heard Dayan Lopian explain that because Moses knew that the concept of hakoras hatov (gratitude) is a fundamental part of God's nature, he understood that any commandment from God to Moses had to be construed in such a way as to make compliance compatible with the principle of hakoras hatov (a little like, l'havdil, the operation of section 3 of the Human Rights Act 1998). Once again, then, the humanity of the Torah depends on giving a construction to its commandments in the context of, and subject to, the fundamental principles of Torah justice as expounded by the rabbis. (As to why the commandment had to be expressed in this way rather than as an express command to send Pinchos, see the Ohr Hachayim on Bamidbar 31:6.) ("The spirit of God hovered over the face of the water" (Bereishis 1:2) – in the case of the Torah, often symbolised by water in aggadic literature, one often finds the spirit of God not apparent on the surface but only after contextual elucidation.)

We can learn two things from this about contemporary inter-faith relations. First, we should remember that the justice and validity of Torah will not always be as apparent to others, who have to rely on the surface text out of context, as it is to us who are able to construe it in the light of tradition and an appreciation of context and background. Secondly, if that is true of Torah it is likely to be true of other religions as well: when terrorists cite as support for their actions blood-curdling passages from the Koran which appear to admit only of a violent and unjust construction, we should be aware that the true clerics of Islam will be as assiduous in putting those passages in their proper context so as to derive a proper meaning from them, as we are in the case of our own religion.

We enter on Sunday the three weeks of mourning for the Temple. The Temple was a universal structure, open to and used by all humankind. And so it will be again. Different traditions and cultures will come together, as we pray on Rosh Hashanah, under the kingship of God as the final stage of a process which can begin only with each applying the most beneficial and generous construction to each other's traditions and actions, and each seeking to find and support the best in each other.

54

The Psychic Octopus
and Torah Codes

It's amazing what people will believe, and neither religious nor secular people seem to have a monopoly of gullibility. (From 8th July 2010)

So Paul the psychic octopus has done it again, correctly predicting Germany's defeat by Spain in the World Cup. Which means, of course, that Paul is a genuinely intelligent and prescient being who is capable of guiding humanity by accurately predicting the future in various ways and doubtless offering all kinds of spiritual and intellectual advice and support.

Or, if you have any sense, it serves as a reminder that given any two, random series of numbers or other data there is a certain percentage chance of correlation and that, given an infinite number of possible combinations of series, it is unsurprising that from time to time we stumble across two series with no substantive connection that correlate randomly.

So back to the Torah codes. If by following the Fibonacci sequence and adding three each time and applying it to the text of the Torah I can produce the sentence "Israel will not succeed unless [insert your own favourite obsession here]" I have proven conclusively either that I am a gullible idiot with too much time on my hands or that I am an unscrupulous obsessive who hopes that other people are gullible idiots with too much time on their hands. I have not, however, proven anything else.

55

Skvering the Circle:
the oppression of Women

One of the biggest distractions in considering Judaism's attitude to women and their role in the religion is the difficulty of separating cultural influences from religious requirements. (From 11th January 2008)

Treating women as unpaid domestic slaves who should be neither seen nor heard is no part of Judaism. It is, however, engrained in the community, being one of the less pleasant habits that we picked up from our various host-cultures over the years; and because it is peculiarly convenient for many of those who shape the nature of religious life it is a habit that we appear reluctant to abandon.

The latest of a stream of Chassidishe Rebbeim is in London – the Skverer Rebbe. Last night a mass gathering of all the primary school children in the area attended upon the Rebbe to receive his blessings – with the small and unimportant exception of those who happen to be female.

Only one school – the Independent Jewish Day School – has bothered to make arrangements for its girls also to attend upon the Rebbe, who is delighted to receive them.

Every other school is, in essence, giving its girls a clear message that they and their spiritual aspirations are insignificant: that they simply do not register on the scale of things that matter. This is not a matter of public ritual in which the performance of public parts is reserved to men, like it or not, as a matter of Jewish law. It is a question of remembering that the spiritual attainments of girls and women are as important as those of boys and men.

One of the few positive things about majority Western cultures today is that women are to a large degree emancipated. Our girls see this, and participate in it in their secular lives. If our religion does not reflect this and keep pace with it – enabling women to be as fulfilled and challenged in their spiritual lives as they are in their secular avocations – girls will vote with their feet and leave the community; and it will be our fault.

56

Reform Judaism –
The Penny Drops

Another aspect of the JFS "Who is a Jew?" case was the unexpectedly equivocal reaction from non-orthodox institutions. The piece below suggested one reason that occurred to me at the time. I suspect I was probably wrong. But at least it's short. (From 3rd February 2008)

A certain Jewish school is being taken to court for refusing admission to a child who is not halachically Jewish, although the child is Jewish according to the Reform movement. So one might expect them to be enthusiastic about the litigation: but they are not at all, because they have realised that once the courts intervene in matters of who is and is not Jewish, there is no guarantee that they will adopt precisely the Reform's criteria – they might substitute their own entirely.

The Talmud noticed something similar a few centuries ago. At the end of the tractate Avodoh Zarah two rabbis are eating in the palace of a non-Jewish king. He insists that one of them is offered all kosher facilities. The other says "What about me?" To which the answer is that the King has been watching this second rabbi's behaviour, and has come to the conclusion that he does not consistently follow one set of rules but makes them up as he goes along to suit his convenience.

We can ask the non-Jewish world to respect our religious practices when they are consistent and sincere, based on adherence to the Code of Jewish Law redacted centuries ago in codification of still earlier authority, based on time-honoured majority practice where opinions originally differed. Once we adopt a do-it-yourself free-for-all attitude where we make the rules up ourselves, they are not worthy of respect and will not receive it.

ISRAEL

57

Shemittah Year and the Heter Mechirah

In many circles, the land and State of Israel appear to be becoming less important to Jewish observance all the time. That is true not only of the peculiar concentrations within the orthodox camp that are theologically opposed to the establishment of the State of Israel. It is simply that many for whom Israel is theoretically important, and who in principle support the establishment of the State of Israel, see it more and more as a convenient centre for tourism and study, and less and less as the ultimate culmination of thousands of years of dreams and hope. When I was growing up, in many households the blue and white JNF charity box was treated with almost as much veneration as the mezuzah on the door post (and the contents were certainly checked more frequently). Perhaps as Israel has become more and more successful materially, and as physical and financial support from the diaspora is less and less relevant to Israeli economic well-being, there is an emerging feeling along the lines of "Well if they don't need us anymore, then we won't need them either".

As well as being profoundly troubling theologically, as the aspiration to a Jewish State is one of the few central concepts of Judaism that has remained consistent since its inception, this is also troubling for another reason: any community that is purely introspective tends to go barking bonkers sooner rather than later, and the potential for that within a religious community is particularly strong and dangerous. Constant association with the diversity of approaches and opinions in Israel, is one way of even a small Jewish community in the diaspora remaining grounded by reference to a variety of ideas. For that reason alone, it is important to embrace anything that enhances our practical points of connection with the land of Israel, and important to avoid anything that tends to distance us from it. (From 27th September 2014)

I attended an excellent shiur on the halochos of shemittah[19] this afternoon.

The issues underpinning the controversy around the heter mechirah were carefully explained.

The conclusion was that for preference heter mechirah produce should be avoided in chutz la'aretz;[20] but that it can certainly be relied upon if necessary, and should not be avoided at the cost of causing offence or creating divisions.

All fine so far as it goes: I would add one thing.

At a time when people are boycotting Israeli goods, many Jews in chutz la'aretz who want to show

---

[19] Sabbatical year.
[20] Outside Israel.

their solidarity for Israel will see buying Israeli goods as one effective way of doing that: and they will certainly want to rely on the heter mechirah for that purpose and will be pleased to know that without doubt they have solid halachic ground on which to rely.

Hopefully this year will bring peace to Israel and the whole world, and we will all be able to support every nation's commercial endeavours in a spirit of universal harmony.

58

How many Chief Rabbis Does
It Take to Light a Candle?

*I wrote the piece below as an immediate answer reaction
to one of my first exposures to a standard Israeli, no
Israeli national religious event. The internal divides
between different classes of orthodoxy continue to char-
acterise is ready society. The former Chief Rabbi Lord,
visits used to observe that before the emergence of religious parties in Israeli politics, the Orthodox community
had no power but considerable influence; and after the
emergence of religious political parties the orthodox community acquired in enormous power and lost all its influence. The chief rubbing it as an institution appears to be
all about internal communal power politics and is nothing
about an attempt to establish a religious institution that
will be of utility to the community and command respect
and influence outside. (From 20th December 2011)*

I was at the Chanukiah lighting at the Kotel this evening,
and very moving it was too – but one aspect of it
brought to the front of my mind a thought that has been
lurking undiscovered in the background for some time.

The Sephardi Chief Rabbi lit the Chanukiah and then spoke, very appropriately and movingly. And when he had finished we were all ready for a bit of dancing. But, of course, we had to have another Chief Rabbi first, for the Ashkenazim. There was nothing in particular for him to add – and the atmosphere was only dampened by his contribution. Then the Minister for Education felt the need to point out at some length that he wasn't planning to give the Kotel back to anyone, which presumably nobody in particular had been expecting him to do today anyway. And then in order to dissipate any remaining fragments of atmosphere, some other random blighter said it all over again.

Then we would have danced, but almost everyone had gone home (including the musician!)

Although it wouldn't have dealt with the Minister and the random blighter, it would have been a much better start to have just the one Chief Rabbi. And it does ring a little hollow to have them standing there going on about the indissoluble unity of the Jewish people when there are two of them!

The Chief Rabbi is not a position that requires sectarian loyalty; indeed, it should be above it. Nor is there any good reason I can think of why we couldn't have just one Chief Rabbi of Israel. For halachic matters where there are differences between Ashkenazi and Sephardi attitudes, he could take advice, as they must have to anyway where there are other variant minhagim. And he could then talk about Jewish unity as if we (as well as he) meant it.

The only possible argument I can think of against having a single Chief Rabbi is that the position is more about politics, influence and control of budgets than it is about religion; and that must be too cynical to be true, mustn't it?!

Happy Chanukah – and roll on a genuinely united Jewish people.

59

Tachanun on
Yom Ha'Atzmaut

As I say in Chapter 57, it troubles me that Israel appears to be becoming less relevant to diaspora Jewish ortho-doxy in many ways. This piece also touches on that, but it goes further: whatever one thinks about the theo-logical, communal or political role of the State of Israel today, roughly half of the Jewish population is living there, a number very roughly equivalent to those exter-minated by the Nazis during the Holocaust. How can we not grieve when they grieve, and rejoice when they rejoice? Can we really treat the day that brings most of Israel to a joyous standstill as a religious irrelevance in the cloistered and self-obsessed introspective compla-cency of Golders Green, Stamford Hill or any other diaspora suburb you like to mention? (From 30th April 2008)

Two years ago, I was giving a citizenship talk to the Hasmonean Girls' School sixth form and we somehow got onto the subject of Yom Ha'Atzmaut and how one celebrates it. A girl at the front announced smugly

"I don't celebrate it at all, because it's in the Omer".[21] I congratulated her on her perspicuity and added that since the Omer restrictions are to commemorate the deaths of Rabbi Akiva's pupils, and since the rabbis attribute the plague that killed them to disunity and in particular the inability to show each other respect while differing on matters of law and philosophy, by ignoring Yom Ha'Atzmaut she was indeed keeping the Omer appropriately by introducing a little more division and disunity into the world.

The vast majority of the observant Jewish world today celebrates Yom Ha'Atzmaut as a modern miracle and a significant spiritual opportunity.

Of course, different communities do it in their different ways, and according to their different halachic understandings. In the matter of Hallel, in particular, opinions vary as to whether and how it is to be said.

To omit Hallel on halachic grounds is for the present just about tenable (although I suspect that in another few years it will have become such a tiny minority opinion as to be practically untenable). But to say Tachanun is another thing altogether.

I brought an Israeli friend with me to shul on Yom Ha'Atzmaut a few years ago. When we got to Tachanun and the rabbi and a few others started to say it he looked at me with shock and disbelief. He could not believe that anywhere outside the deliberately isolationist communities of the chareidim Tachanun would be said on Yom Ha'Atzmaut, and our community, while

---

[21] The period between Passover and Shavuot during which some restrictions of public celebration are observed.

nominally part of the Adas, does not have the appearance of a chareidi shul.

The general tzibbur of Jews in Eretz Yisroel celebrates Yom Ha'Atzmaut as a yom tov akin to Purim and Chanukah. The din of *al tifrosh min hatzibbur* (do not separate yourself from the community) comes into play at a global level as well as at an individual level. It takes little to defer Tachanun: a private simchah such as a bris is enough to prevent an entire community from saying Tachanun: the simchah of 6 million Jews in Israel should be enough to prevent Tachanun from being said by the rest of the worldwide community (apart from the fact that even for those of us who do not presently live in Israel, the State and its foundation are of enormous spiritual significance).

60

Disengagement from Gaza

Whatever one thinks about the political rights and wrongs, and the security implications, of the forced evacuation of the Jewish settlements in Gaza, the use of the Israeli army to dispossess Jewish families of their homes caused major trauma throughout Israeli society and has left scars that may never fully heal. I have never understood enough about Israeli politics to form a view about issues of this kind, but I was in Israel during part of the disengagement, and it left me with vivid images discussed in this piece. (From 29th August 2005)

Having returned a few hours ago from spending the past four weeks in Israel I wish to mention, by way of an interim communication before the next planned issue of the Sceptic Tank, the two most powerful images which have stayed in my mind from all the things I saw and heard about the disengagement.

There are two texts of the poem "El adon" which we sing on shabbos morning just after bor'chu. One has the phrase "chessed v'rachamim lifnei k'vodo" (kindness and mercy precede His glory) and the other has the phrase "chessed v'rachamim molei k'vodo" (His glory is filled with kindness and mercy). Each is used, by those praying according to different customs.

As always when two texts have survived in mainstream use, it is because there is merit in each. The first version is along the lines of the famous saying "derech eretz kodmo laTorah" (good behaviour precedes Torah). Before one attempts to aspire to the Divine one must master the humane: one cannot become holy without first being a thoroughly decent human being. The second version stresses that the values of kindness and mercy are not just prerequisites for holiness but that they also permeate, and are inseparable from, Divine behaviour (which is why Abraham could say to God about Sodom "choliloh lecho …" – "it is inconceivable for you to behave in such a way as to kill the innocent".

I saw both these texts exemplified in the sight of two Jews approaching each other on apparently irreconcilable courses destined for violent collision; a Jewish soldier bound by his understanding of Torah and secular law to evict a resident, and a resident bound by his understanding of Torah to resist the secular law of eviction so far as possible without infringing any Torah commandment. (As to why dina d'malchuso may not make observing the secular law a Torah requirement in this case, if there is a sufficient demand I will bli neder address this on another occasion). The resident's behaviour towards the soldier showing dignity and understanding for the other's position, and vice versa: a profound sensitivity for each other showing that the Torah of each is based on a profound humanity, and that his or her religious observance is also imbued with and permeated by sensitivity. The soldier lifts the resident carefully and respectfully and carries him out of the house: the resident is careful not to harm the solider who lifts him, and utters not even a word of protest, only cries; and when he is placed carefully on the ground outside his former home, the two cry together.

I do not know whether you saw these images here, or only the occasional tyre being burned in the streets by a hot-headed youth who was probably not even a resident of Gaza. But it is the former images and not the latter which remain in my mind, as a picture of inspiring behaviour and a testament to Jewish values. Let the politics of the situation be what they may, and even leaving aside how one construes Torah obligations in the matters of settling the land of Israel and of obeying commands, a religion that teaches both sides of a bitter conflict to behave in this fashion to one another is clearly both founded on and imbued with principles of humanity and divinity inextricably entwined.

Of course, not all residents of Gush Katif decided that it was necessary to be carried out of their homes; and my second most powerful memory of the past month is of being told by one of our friends in Israel that his uncle had been told by his rabbi that it was forbidden to leave in advance, forbidden to pack even the day before, but that in order to avoid loss of dignity and even a risk of violence the family should wait until the police were actually coming towards their house, so that the evacuation was for all practical purposes at last inevitable, and then stand up and walk out with dignity.

We all suffer losses throughout our lives – most are relatively trivial although irksome enough at the time, and some unhappily are truly tragic. I have no idea what the political or security message of the disengagement process is; but I think the principal religious message for me is clear: to try to learn to suffer loss – and where necessary to inflict loss – with dignity, sensitivity and humility.

61

Tefilas Tal – Last Chance for Israeli Society

Since I wrote this piece the furore over drafting the so-called "ultra" religious communities into the Israeli army has thundered on, with occasional outbreaks of unrest. For me, the stubborn refusal to consider national service is the strongest proof that those communities are entirely without any form of effective, intelligent and principled leadership. (From 1st August 2012)

As the Tal law exempting religious ("Chareidi") Jews in Israel from military service finally expires amid confusion as to what will succeed it, I declare an interest. My younger son is a strictly-orthodox Jew: he follows the Code of Jewish Law as meticulously as anyone in the Chareidi community, and his rabbis are as pious and learned as anyone in the Chareidi community. He emigrated to Israel last summer and has already been signed up for military service, although he could have avoided it pretty much forever had he chosen to.

But my son prefers to be able to look himself in the face in the morning than to avoid army service.

If you live in a country where the borders need guarding, then you take your turn in guarding them: otherwise, what are you but a coward and a parasite, living off the efforts of others?

The argument that one often hears – that by studying in yeshivah a boy does more to invoke divine protection of Israel than any soldier can achieve – holds good for a tiny minority of boys who are such devoted and successful scholars that not one man or woman in Israel would wish to disturb their studies, or would think them more useful in the army than in the yeshivah. By definition, however, these boys will have the humility not to see themselves as anything special, and they will wish to take their turn in the army along with everyone else, and will have to be restrained.

Anyone who protests that he is too good or too holy for the army proves the falseness of the proposition by making it.

As to the suggestion that army life will corrupt boys, it is either complete nonsense or a horrendous indictment of the Chareidi educational system that needs to be corrected whether or not their boys go into the army.

Israel has stumbled by blind degrees into a situation that would now be farcical if it were not so tragic. Boys hiding behind their religious books in order to evade army service don't damage the army, but they threaten the nature and future of Israel as a Jewish State, which can be justified only when all Jews present a united front, held together by love and respect for each other, with our cultural and religious differences simply enhancing our overall unity.

If I were a non-religious Israeli today, I would hate Judaism. I would look at the many tens of thousands of

Jews who tell each other how superior they are to me, and live a life characterised by cowardice. I would see the orthodox boys who come from abroad to learn in yeshivah, and whose wives become immigrants in order to collect welfare benefits while they themselves remain foreign-nationals in order to evade army service; and I would be disgusted with them, with their rabbis who allow it, and with their God in whose name it is done.

The crisis over the Tal law has little or nothing to do with the army, but it has everything to do with the health of the nation. For those of us who believe that God protects Israel and the Jewish people only while they deserve protection, finding a solution that allows the Chareidi world to recover its self-respect by playing a full and equal part in society is the last chance.

62

Yehudah, Beit Shemesh, the Chief Rabbi, the Pope and Responsibility

Another rant about the importance of individual responsibility ... (From 31ˢᵗ December 2011)

Since my post saying that the Chief Rabbi is wrong in telling the Pope that religion is the answer to restoring the "soul" to Europe, I have been wondering what is the answer.

Since my post about the nutters in Beit Shemesh shouting at little girls in the name of religion, I have been watching the media discussing who is really to blame.

Last night my son Yisroel gave an excellent shiur on the week's parashah, Vayigash, at the end of which he focused on the fact that the word "vayigash" emphasises that Yehudah finally steps forward to accept personal responsibility for his brothers' welfare and thereby justifies his hereditary position of leadership.

Personal responsibility seems to me to be the key to lots of things.

In one of the *Father Brown* stories G.K. Chesterton has the priest comment on the use of early lie-detectors; he says they are as useless as the medieval idea that a murder suspect is made to touch the corpse and if blood flows it is a sign of guilt: "Blood flows, fast or slow, in dead folk or living, for so many more million reasons than we can ever know. Blood will have to flow very funnily; blood will have to flow up the Matterhorn, before I will take it as a sign that I am to shed it." This reminded me of an old post of mine entitled "What if God's a Christian?"[22] (which annoyed a few people), the essential thesis of which was that I should live on the assumption that my religious beliefs might be wrong, and avoid doing anything that, without religion, I would have to be ashamed of. Father Brown's refusal to shed blood based on belief in superstition or trust in machinery is an assertion of personal responsibility for his actions – neither religion nor anything else should be used as a cover or excuse for my own action or inaction.

So (1): the "soul" of Europe will be restored when children, and adults, are taught how and why to take personal responsibility for their actions.

And so (2): the real problem of Beit Shemesh is that 30 malicious nutters are being allowed by 10,000 passive chareidi residents to taint the chareidi reputation, because the 10,000 are failing to accept personal responsibility for the need to do anything positive to protect children from being abused in their name.

---

[22] See Chapter 1.

63

Beit Shemesh Beastliness:
Two Questions and an early
New Year's Resolution

*It's odd that ultra-orthodox communities who look
down on the merely orthodox as beyond the pale still
consider us fit to approach for charitable donations;
what is even odder is that we habitually donate ...
(From 11th September 2011)*

Watching YouTube clips of so-called chareidim lining
up in the last few weeks and days to bellow bestially at
young girls going to and from school – in protest at
their holy neighbourhood (which the school isn't in)
being sullied by the immodesty of short socks for five-
year olds, has made me ask myself two questions and
form an early pre-Rosh Hashanah resolution.

Question No. 1: How can these people seriously
think that behaving like this is consistent with adherence to anything worth calling a religion?

Question No.2: If these men are meant to be chassidim, where are their Rebbeim, why don't they know

what their followers are up to, and if they do know it why don't they or can't they stop it?

New Year's Resolution: Bli neder, I do not intend to give a single penny to any individual or organisation who asks for charity unless and until they sign the following declaration with which I will present them—

> "I unequivocally condemn the behaviour of those so-called chareidim who bellow bestially at the schoolgirls of Orot, Beit Shemesh on their way to and from school; I acknowledge that this behaviour demonstrates appalling moral delinquency and utter spiritual bankruptcy; and I encourage this declaration, with my signature, to be brought to the attention of those gedolei Torah who are meant to be the leaders of these disgusting animals."

Those seeking a donation will have to sign the declaration and append their names, addresses and sectarian affiliation.

64

Yeshivah Inspections – Points of View

People often ask, "How can people who claim to be orthodox Jews fiddle their taxes or get involved in money-laundering?" The question misses the point: it is precisely <u>because</u> these people claim to be orthodox Jews that they come to think themselves above the rules that apply to the rest of us. (From 31st July 2011)

Last week's Hamodiah carries an indignant out-pouring about the enormities inflicted on the yeshivah world by two Government inspectors who arrived in the middle of a rosh yeshivah's shiur and attempted to insist on verifying the students at once without waiting for the end of the shiur. They were ejected by zealous students, the rosh yeshivah complained to the Government, and at least one meeting was organised at which the yeshivah world erupted into a self-righteous hysterical frenzy of scandalised victim-hood.

The Torah-true response to the incident would, of course, have been upon the following lines.

"What a disgrace it is for the Torah world that by the crooked behaviour of a number of so-called yeshivahs in claiming Government grants for non-existent students the Government has entirely reasonably found it necessary to inflict upon us the shame of having our claims verified by inspection of attendances; what a lesson this humiliation should be for us that by purporting to be orthodox and learned Jews our behaviour should be beyond reproach or we heap insults on the Torah itself; let us at least try to restore our self-respect as a community, and a perception of decency in the eyes of others, by cooperating with the inspectors in a humble and helpful fashion; and, in particular, let us not waste even more of the public money by keeping the inspectors waiting just because we happen to be in the middle of learning – learning can wait, but re-establishing the honour of the yeshivah community cannot."

Simples?

GENERAL RELIGIOUS ISSUES

65

The Pope and
Good Manners

There is a tendency in some communities for the idea of manners or courtesy to be belittled or even ridiculed, and consigned to some kind of stereotypical Victorian past of stiffness and artificially elaborate social norms. Jews are, in particular, fond of observing that manners are a very English thing, and that Israelis don't really have any. A very brief journey to Israel is enough to expose this as the obvious nonsense that it sounds like. It is true that Israeli manners are different from English manners; or, rather, that the different communities within Israel have a range of different social conventions that vary from many of the different ranges of social conventions within English communities. But every society has its rules and conventions which polite people observe and rude people ignore. And between all communities there are certain shared values that should mean, for example, that anybody could work out that displaying an undignified photograph of a visitor to your country is in poor taste. Manners may not be the most important thing in the world; but since they are the beginning of good *relations between different families, communities and nationalities, they are not so unimportant either. (From 16th September 2010)*

Scottish atheists are welcoming the Pope with a special "Good Without God" protest.

I know of no religion (including Judaism) that denies the ability to be a good person without religious belief.

The more important question, however, seems to be whether people, religious or not, can bring themselves to behave decently nowadays, by the exertion of a modicum of common sense and self-control.

The journalists who managed to catch a photograph of the Pope with his face covered by his own shawl in the wind doubtless thought "what a scoop"; that is a reasonable first thought – but the second thought should have been "come to think of it, though, not very kind to publish such an undignified picture – let's just quietly bin it".

Similarly, whether or not atheists are right, might not sheer good manners lead one to think that a billboard denying God is an impolite welcome to Scotland?

And the Cardinal expressing trenchant views about secularism in Britain may or may not have been airing an important issue, but simple good manners might have suggested that this was not the time, place or manner in which to do it.

Perhaps we are all so busy nowadays being right, and fervent in our protestations of how right we are, that we forget to be well-mannered.

I don't know who first said "manners maketh man", but it has something to be said for it: manners are more than a superficial social etiquette – they are part of our instinctive knowledge of what is good and bad behaviour that forms part of the Divine image in which some of us believe we were created.

The Pope has plenty of policy and religious issues to address (and so far as I can see he does not seem to be an unhelpfully complacent or self-satisfied personality): but there is a time and a place for everything – he is the head of a religion to which a few millions of our fellow human-beings belong, and we owe it to ourselves to give him a welcome that exudes human warmth and a respect for human dignity.

66

The Chief Rabbi, the Pope and the Soul of Europe

Religious leaders still seem oblivious to the fact that organised religion is causing infinitely more hate and hate anger and damage in the world than anything else. Interfaith events often central around a shared belief in the importance of having some kind of religious conviction. That is one of the reasons why I wish we had fewer interfaith events, and a great deal more interpersonal events where ordinary human beings, without any financial or other vested interest in the propagation of dogma or the increase of religious commitments, could reassert shared human values based on nothing else than A belief in humanity. There is so much precious about human instinct that can be celebrated, whether one believes that it is a random whether one believes that it has been created by random events of nature or the guiding her Hand of a single God, or indeed in any other way. (From 18th December 2011)

According to *the Jewish Chronicle*, in the Chief Rabbi's lecture at the Pontifical Gregorian University he said:

"When a civilisation loses its faith, it loses its future. When it recovers its faith, it recovers its future. For the sake of our children, and their children not yet born, we – Jews and Christians, side-by-side – must renew our faith and its prophetic voice. We must help Europe rediscover its soul."

It strikes me that this is about as inappropriate a moment as one could find for it to be suggested that all that Europe needs to rediscover its soul is co-operation between the Catholic church and institutionalised Judaism.

Organised religion in general seems to be doing as much as any other force in today's world to sow the seeds of dissension and violence. While the Catholic church has particularly acute present crises of conscience, all the major religions about which I know anything at all seem to be contributing more to the sum total of human misery than to the sum total of human happiness.

The Chief Rabbi is undoubtedly right that Europe – and not just Europe – is in moral crisis, and to describe that as needing to rediscover the soul is entirely apt. Hundreds of thousands of people of all ages are desperately in need of moral direction and focus; and the lack of these is leaving a horrendous mark on the development of societies throughout the world.

But what these people need is not a new gang to belong to, or a new dogma to excuse intolerance and thuggery; rather they need help to rediscover the inherent appreciation of moral values that are the image of God in which we are all created. All religions worthy of the name – and many non-religious philosophies and approaches to life – are capable at a personal level of reigniting a human being's spark of holiness; but organised religion, as distinct from personal religion, is as in need as anyone else of rediscovering its soul; and until it has healed itself it will not be ready to be part of the solution rather than an exacerbation of the problem.

67

The Two-Faith Solution

I am generally a little suspicious of interfaith events and projects, partly for reasons explored in other pieces in this book. Contact between faiths at official level by dialogue between those who hold themselves out as representatives of the faiths, is generally both superficial and somewhat disingenuous. Is it entirely honest to spend an afternoon complimenting a synagogue on its architecture and the forms and practices of its worship, and then go home to pray for the consignment of unbelievers in a particular form of Christianity to eternal damnation? But whatever the limitations on "official" dialogue between religions, all communication at a human level between different human beings has the potential to advance the cause of peace for all, and is therefore strongly to be encouraged. As part of that, and in order to support informed and constructive contact between people of different religions, a little bit of advance information about those other religions is, one should have thought, only to be welcomed. Surprising, therefore, how apparently open-minded and generally ecumenical religious leaders can be opposed to their followers being educated in religious matters beyond the confines of their own religion. (From 24th September 2014)

The Government's proposal that students of GCSE Religious Studies would each have to show evidence of having studied two faiths has apparently united all faith groups in the UK in furious opposition.

What a shame.

In the Rosh Hashanah prayers tomorrow, we repeatedly proclaim God's kingship over the whole world – it is a universalist message, with very little about the Jewish people in it and a continual concentration on the challenges and opportunities of humanity.

All around the world today we see religion being used as an excuse for the worst kinds of evil (including that particularly dangerous and insidious evil – simple indifference to others' feelings, needs and sufferings).

And all around the world we see that evil combated by simple humanity, expressing itself in a variety of forms and manners, some religious, some ethical, some pure – unlabelled – human instinct.

The Rosh Hashanah liturgy celebrates the universality of the human condition – its weaknesses and its strengths.

Why deny children the opportunity to do the same, just because they happen to be studying a GCSE?

This is not a proposal for compulsory religious education for anyone; merely a proposal that if your own religion is important enough to you to be worth basing one of your school qualifications on, and if you would like that qualification to be recognised in the form of a public examination, you should accept the public's wish to enhance your citizenship potential by simply learning a little bit about what motivates some of the other human beings with whom you share the world, and with whom you share most or all of the characteristics that shape and drive your own spiritual journey.

Sounds like a good idea to me – and hopefully a recipe for a happy new year for us all.

68

Cartoons

What is and is not offensive is of course massively cultur-
ally variable. We all know that a hand gesture that in one
culture is unexceptionable may be a horrendously crass
insult in another culture. The big question, however, is
whether offence should be "in the eye of the beholder" or
a question of intent. If in my culture it is normal to
lampoon religious sensibilities in cartoons, and I am
innocent of all intention to offend but am exercising my
accepted right to free speech, do you have a right to take
offence because if a person in your culture did the same
thing they would be assumed to have the intention to
offend? And even if you do have the right to take
offence, does that necessarily come with a corresponding
duty not to give offence. New questions that the world is
grappling with very fast in the light of certain strains in
Islam. (From 5th February 2006)

A few thoughts on the Torah reaction to the events of
the last few days around the publication of cartoon cari-
catures of the Islamic prophet Mohammed.

The concept that "sticks and stones may break my
bones but words will never harm me" is not in

accordance with Torah thought. The rabbis have always taught us to be aware of the power, constructive and destructive, of words. A life can be ruined as effectively by a few words spoken at the right time and place as by a blow.

The Torah has a concept of blasphemy that imposes obligations even on those who do not subscribe to our religion. One of the seven Noachide laws – incumbent in Torah thought on all humans – is a fairly extensive prohibition against idolatry. There is nothing ideologically tolerant about Judaism.

In order to become liable for a penalty in respect of blasphemy, however, a person has to perform it, after clear warning, with clear knowledge and intent; not out of mere ignorance or even out of gross discourtesy. Although there is one notable instance of extra-judicial punishment of blasphemy – that carried out by Pinchos[23] – as a general rule an infringement of the Noachide laws can be punished only through the usual judicial channels.

Collective punishment is in theory contrary to Torah law. There are, however, some instances – whether general categories such as the city given over to idolatry, or specific historical examples such as the punishment inflicted by Shimon and Levi in the matter of Dinah's maltreatment – that illustrate that the concept is not unknown to Torah law, in certain circumstances.

All of which puts us in perhaps a slightly ambivalent position in respect of the present crisis. We can certainly understand the strength of feeling that religious

---

[23] See also Chapter 53 – *Pinchos and terrorism.*

Muslims will feel upon seeing a disrespectful picture published in a form that contravenes their law. And we are not inclined to dismiss it as "mere words or pictures", being aware of the force that words and pictures can command. But we feel deep antipathy towards any scene of mass hysterical violence, of a kind which would not be justified in Torah thought by any breach of Torah law. We also feel, and are required to practice, an innate respect for the law of the land, even in some cases (but admittedly not all) where that law diverges from Torah law.

It seems, unhappily, likely that we are all going to have to develop at greater speed than had previously been thought our ideas about ways to achieve balance between inherently incompatible ways of life. Not only will we find incompatibilities between cultures, but within our own we will find, as is shown above, principles which can be difficult to apply compatibly in a particular situation. As with most difficult projects, however, if it is undertaken by all those for whom it is necessary with a genuine wish to arrive at a solution which provides the greatest ease of mind to all, we can hope with God's help to achieve a result which will certainly be better than mere reaction by instinct to each new class of culture.

69

Electronic Christmas
Cards – Missing the Point

*Commercialisation of Christmas is widely decried –
I'm much more worried about the electrification of
Christmas ... (From 19th December 2007)*

As an orthodox Jew, it is always comforting to see that
most religions get most things wrong in most of the
same ways.

For the past few years on the Jewish festival of Purim
the pleasing law of exchanging small edible gifts has
been eroded by the advent of a crop of smug little cards,
saying things along the lines of "We think there is too
much waste involved in giving mishloach monos[24] – so
we have given charity on your behalf instead."

It is wonderful to give charity. But it is not the point
of Purim gifts. The point of them is to show that before
tucking into my own delightful Purim meal I have
thought about what my friends and family will have for
theirs. I also have to think about those without enough

---

[24] Presents of food, given to each other on Purim.

to eat at all – and there is an entirely separate duty of giving money to charity on Purim itself. It is not about spending lots of money on food that will be wasted (so the Talmud states that in some cases exchanging meals is the best answer): but it is about thinking of my friends and translating my thoughts into actions that will enhance their pleasure and comfort.

Christmas cards used to have the same idea. As I wandered among my colleagues' offices I would see piles of cards, showing that people were thinking of each other at this time of year and translating that into action: now I see far fewer – they have been largely replaced by smug little electronic messages which swamp the ether along the lines of "We are saving the planet by not sending out any Christmas cards this year".

There is no point in having a planet at all if we are going to make it as miserable and devoid of comfort as possible. Christmas cards are important. They translate thoughts into action and show people with whom we may have little contact the rest of the year that they matter to us enough not merely to add them to a copy list of a row of smug electronic dots, but enough to take a card, find a picture they will appreciate, write a message that will brighten their day, and go along to the Post Office to send it.

Religions of the world: unite against the de-personalisation of human relationships!

70

Christmas without God – the Jewish Objection to Harry Potter

It took me a long time to work out what troubled me about the scene of Hagrid dragging a huge Christmas tree through the Great Hall in the first Harry Potter film ... (From 4th December 2007)

As soon as I had recovered from denouncing Harry Potter as derivative tripe (i.e. as soon as I stopped talking about it and started reading it) I found it a powerful and absorbing work, with a moral tone that generally made it ideal escapist literature to fill the odd hour or two in the bath. But after a while something started to bother me, and as the bubble bath subsided I worked out what it was.

Harry Potter is the ultimate secular novel. It sanitises morality and attempts to divorce it entirely from any kind of religious tradition. It is, in fact, the second important literary work which is all about good and evil and manages to avoid all mention of God. We have Christmas scenes – without God. We have a portrayal of the after-life – without God. We have all kinds of ethical and moral issues – without God.

The other major literary work that studiously avoids the G-word is the Book of Esther in the Bible. But rabbinic tradition has it that although the name of God is absent, every time the word "The King" (one word in Hebrew) appears, it is to be read as referring both to King Achashverosh and, in some way, to God. The point is that while the story operates at a secular level, God is never far away. He is hovering underneath every line of the story, and challenging the characters to find Him in their everyday lives. And the characters seek Him out through prayer in the dark times and acknowledge His kindness by showing kindness to each other in the good times.

Jewish thought teaches us to trust in humans only in so far as their moral instincts derive from the imagery of God in which we were created. To guide and fashion those instincts we need to look for God all the time, trying to find different ways of uncovering His influences in the world and enhancing His influence on our lives. We should not try to write Him out of the story, abandoning long-standing religious traditions for pure secular self-reliance.

71

Electronic Goats and Indoor Succahs

It's nice to see that all religions have similar problems. Islam and Judaism are particularly similar in both having a mass of relatively complex and technical laws, a situation which inevitably tempts the ingenious to find ways to keep the letter of the law in circumstances where it might otherwise be impossible or inconvenient to do so. Which immediately gives rise to the question of whether there is a spirit to a particular law and, if so, whether a particular technical solution to complying with the letter of the law fails to satisfy that spirit. The piece below highlights an issue in Islamic religious law that struck an immediate chord of similarity when I read about it. (From 10th January 2006)

Today is Eid al-Adha, the Islamic day of sacrifice. One of the observances of the day is a requirement to have an animal slaughtered and to donate the meat to the poor. There will be many Muslims who are more than happy to make this financial sacrifice but who find it difficult or impossible to spend the necessary time purchasing and delivering an animal. So a scheme has been made available in Jakarta whereby customers of a local bank may use its automatic machines to buy an animal (at costs starting at about £40 for a goat) following which all the necessary arrangements are made electronically and the purchaser eventually receives photographs of the slaughtered animal and a letter of thanks from the community which receives the meat. The BBC asked a "senior Muslim leader" whether he thought the electronic purchase satisfied the requirements of Eid: his reported reply was that "it was in accordance with Islam, but ... unless you witnessed the slaughter first-hand and donated the meat personally, the religious experience would never be the same".

This last sentiment appears to me to be both perfectly expressed and capable of application to a variety of observances in a variety of religions. Perhaps particularly for Jews because of the multitude or religious observances of various kinds required from us daily, there is always a temptation to look for ways of facilitating compliance with ritual laws. Nor is this necessarily to be criticised in itself: on the contrary, anything which enables or encourages more people to participate more fully in their religion is to be welcomed.

But there is a price to pay, and it is important to be realistic. One can see how physically acquiring an animal, supervising its slaughter and handing it over to a soup kitchen to be cooked and distributed, for example, could be a spiritual experience of profound impact. It could make a person more appreciative of his or her blessings of wealth and more sensitive to the needs of others; and different people would doubtless be affected in different ways. It would be much more difficult to draw the same kind of spiritual inspiration from the action of pausing for a few seconds to purchase an electronic goat: not necessarily impossible, but inevitably more difficult. Of course, a person who could not or would not fulfil this requirement any other way, is gaining by the electronic method more than he or she is losing: and a person who by the electronic method is able to give more than he or she could or would be able to give actually may be gaining spiritually by that consideration more than is lost by the unreality of the electronic method. But there is a balance to be struck, and the important thing is to be honest with oneself in striking it.

A good example of the application of this issue in Judaism would be the indoor succah. Once, the standard practice in this country was to construct something more or less rickety in the garden. Nowadays, more and more people have extensions or other parts of their house with removable roof panels, enabling Succos to be experienced without sacrificing carpeting, furniture, space, comfort or even, to a degree, heating. Again, it is indisputable that this fulfils the halachic requirements. But what about the religious experience? This is an intensely personal matter, a balance which each Jew must strike for himself or herself. Some will conclude that the difficulty of keeping Succos in any other way means that the spiritual gains clearly outweigh the losses. The elderly and infirm, for example, may be enabled through the use of an indoor succah to keep a mitzvoh from which they would otherwise be exempt, shut out from a spiritual experience which they have perhaps found particularly uplifting in other years. But for others, the annual experience of building a personal commemoration of the exodus from

Egypt (not forgetting the fact that there is one Talmudic opinion that the process of building the succah deserves its own brochoh) is an integral part of the process and one which can be either a moving experience or an ineffable nuisance, depending at least in part on how one perceives it.

We must avoid becoming so habituated to the use of technological and other advances to facilitate religious observance that we come routinely to adopt the least burdensome route, without making a personal calculation on each occasion whether the facility dilutes the religious experience unnecessarily and undesirably.

ENVIRONMENT

72

Australia's "Biblical" Floods

As the world shrinks, we have increasingly little excuse for just ignoring natural and man-made disasters as being outside our world; but what sense can we make of them? (From 3rd January 2011)

Australian politicians have been describing Queensland's floods as being of "Biblical" proportions.

With the size of area that has been devastated, there will certainly be hundreds or thousands of people who look around and see their entire world as having been swept away in the floods, and it is only to be expected that they may equate today's floods with the Biblical flood with which God destroyed the world.

Of course, that episode ends with God's promise not to destroy the world again by flood, and there may be many people today who regard that promise as having been broken by recent events. The same would have been true of many victims of the Pakistan floods last year.

There is a simple answer to accusations that God's promise has been broken: the promise was only not to destroy the whole world, and there was no promise not to destroy part of it.

That answer is as unsatisfactory as it is simple: if my entire village, every town I ever visited and all or most of my family have been destroyed by flood, how impressed am I going to be by being told that God's promise is kept because Hendon is still okay?

It reminds me of Cecilia Jupe's answer to the schoolmaster in *Hard Times*, that if one sailor in a hundred is drowned at sea the percentage of losses is 100%, if you happen to be that sailor's mother.

To put it another way, why should it matter to an Australian or Pakistani flood victim whether or not Hendon is still unaffected by the flood?

And the answer to that, of course, is that it depends on how the inhabitants of Hendon behave towards the flood.

If we simply ignore it, or get a transient thrill out of watching it on the television or computer, then our survival is irrelevant to the victims, and so far as they are concerned God's promise not to destroy the world has been broken for all practical purposes.

But if we exert ourselves to reach out to victims of the floods, in all the various ways open to us in today's shrinking world, then they can suddenly see the point of the promise that natural disasters will always leave some people in a position to help the victims. God's promise is meaningful only if we supply the meaning by committing ourselves to exert ourselves. The rainbow that symbolises God's promise not to renew the Biblical flood arches through the sky, and I cannot see for certain where it begins and ends – but that doesn't stop me from setting off in the direction it shows to look for people who might need my help.

We do not understand how or why natural disasters occur. But we can understand that they are challenges and opportunities to assert universal brotherhood.

73

Question: Evolution

I received a few answers to this piece that were clearly intended to be helpful, although I didn't find them so; more remarkably, I didn't receive any troll-like abuse, which must be as strong a tribute as any to how few people have ever read my blog. Although none of the answers seem worth printing, I reproduce the question here by way of celebrating how dense I really am. (From 24th February 2008)

This is a genuine – not rhetorical – question about the scientific theories of evolution (much of many of which is compatible with Torah thought). It will display my complete scientific ignorance – but it may be possible for someone reading this to explain in easy lay terms what it is I want to know.

If the process of evolution from micro-organisms to intelligent life was a completely natural one, why did some organisms only get to animal stage and then stop, while others went through the animal stage to become human? Or, if no species has stopped evolving, is it thought that all species will eventually evolve human intelligence, and if so why are some doing it so much slower than others?

Perhaps even the question doesn't make sense in scientific terms and just shows how little I understand about the theories of evolution: but if it is possible for anyone to offer me a (polite) answer I will be very grateful. Please use the comment bar.

74

Passive Smoking

A key injunction in the Torah is to look after one's health. Participating in activities known to be dangerous is expressly prohibited by Jewish law. So how can the enormous number of apparently orthodox Jews who smoke defined themselves against the charge of blatant hypocrisy? They can't. (From 15th February 2006)

Last night, the House of Commons voted to ban smoking in public places including all pubs, clubs and restaurants. In effect, while smoking tobacco remains lawful in the United Kingdom, we are moving towards a position in which to expose others to what it is known as passive smoking is unlawful.

The rabbis once thought that smoking was good for you (Pnei Yehoshuah Shabbos 39b). Even since everyone has known that it is harmful, the rabbis have consistently refused, for sound reasons, to declare a general prohibition against smoking by those already addicted (Igros Moshe Yoreh Deoh 2:49 and Choshen Mishpot 2:76), although they have consistently declared it forbidden to begin to acquire the habit.

The halachic line on passive smoking is, in the state of medical evidence available today, absolutely clear. Even if there remains some room for a person to choose to continue to expose himself or herself to the certain harm that results from smoking, there are no possible grounds on which I can choose to inflict harm on someone else. Since even in small measures there is actual and quantifiable harm caused by inhaling tobacco smoke, it is forbidden to expose a non-smoker to smoke.

At least one rosh yeshivah of world-wide fame moved several years ago to ban smoking from his beis midrash (Harav Moshe Shternbuch, Teshuvos v'Hanhagos 1:159).

If in any community smoking is openly tolerated, and youngsters are permitted or even encouraged to acquire the habit, one can be certain by this that the community in question does not conduct itself entirely in accordance with the laws and principles of the Torah, whatever other appearances may be to the contrary and whatever other merits and virtues the community may have.

75

Environmental Disruption

As I note elsewhere, the orthodox Jewish community appears all too often to regard environmental issues as being of little or no importance, somehow beneath the notice of those who have more rarefied spiritual matters to focus on. But classic Jewish sources lay considerable stress on environmental awareness, and can suggest some significant modern implications. (From 25th September 2005)

In news reports of natural disasters or of changes in the world (hurricanes, drought, flood, soil erosion, species-extinction and the increasing incidence of asthma and allergies, to name a random selection) it is frequently suggested that the disaster or change – or its severity, rate or impact – is partly a result of the way humans are using the planet and its resources. Some of these suggestions may be unfounded, but probably not all of them. Certainly, there seems little doubt that we are increasingly feeling the effects in numerous ways of courses of action begun decades ago; effects that were to some extent at least wholly unpredictable at the beginning of the process.

An aspect of the Torah approach to the protection of our natural environment emerges from a technical law in yesterday's parashah about the construction of the altar in the Tabernacle.

In Devorim 27:5-6 the Torah says "You shall build a stone altar for God there, without using iron on the stones. Build the altar for God with whole stones ..." Apart from the internal redundancy within that passage, the entire passage is a repetition of the law already given in Shemos 20:22. If it is repeated here in Devorim we can look for a message for a people making the transition from living under miraculous divine protection in the desert to managing and using the natural resources of a fertile and inhabitable land.

When the law against using iron to hew the altar stones is given the first time, Rashi brings an explanation from the Mishnah in Middos (3:4): iron was created to shorten life, and the altar was created to prolong life. The obvious difficulty with this is that iron has potential for construction as well as for destruction, and the same is true of stone. Moreover, the Mishnah goes on to record (3:5) that some of the fittings of the altar were required to be made from iron.

But one important difference in the environmental impact of iron and stone as building materials is suggested by the way in which the law against using iron to hew the altar stones is expressed the second time around. The Netziv analyses the internal redundancies of the verses and concludes that we are first obliged to choose stones that are without irregularities that might tempt us to cut them with iron, and secondly, we are prohibited from using iron on those stones at any stage in the building process.

The result was, as the Mishnah in Middos records, that the builders went to Beit Kerem and dug for stones, selecting only those of precisely the required size and shape, rather than quarrying large quantities of rock from the nearest place, cutting to size and discarding the waste. They used a more laborious process, slower and more expensive, but one that was less environmentally disruptive; searching for existing resources that suit the task rather than violently forcing the natural resources to conform to our requirements. That is a choice that was relevant only in the context of the use of stone. When it comes to the use of iron and other metals, one has no choice but to interfere considerably with the natural world – and with potentially far-reaching and unpredictable consequences – in order to extract the metal and adapt it for use.

The picture that emerges is this: the Torah certainly allows and encourages us to use the whole range of the world's resources for our purposes. When iron is required for fittings of the altar that have to be stronger and more flexible than stone, we should use iron. But when there is a choice of technique and one is less environmentally disruptive than the other, we should use the less disruptive process, even if more demanding or less advantageous in other ways.

We are becoming increasingly aware both that the ecological impact of our actions is unpredictable and also that in many ways we may have progressed too far wholly to avoid undesirable effects of actions long past. But in so far as the future of the planet lies in our hands, we can learn from the Torah laws of the stone for the altar the importance of wherever possible adopting an attitude of humility, so that in harnessing natural resources we interfere with the world as little as possible.

The practical implications of this philosophy could be immense. They might point, for example, to maximising opportunities to harness natural sources of sustainable power-generation rather than relying almost entirely on the oil, gas and nuclear power. It could also be relevant to choices between expensive and laborious irrigation systems to tackle third-world drought and the use of genetic modification to produce greater quantities of food in the developed world that can then be transported to areas of famine. And in smaller ways too, this approach may suggest actions of all kinds, including personal contributions to environmental sensitivity such as recycling – in which context, what a great blessing and opportunity for kiddush hashem[25] it is that the London Borough of Hackney have now appointed two members of the Jewish community to act as community recycling officers.

At a more abstract level, adjusting our view of the world along these lines could lead to a general desire to adapt more to the environment around us, to curb our desires to control and change, and generally to approach the new year in an attitude of greater humility and sensitivity.

---

[25] Sanctification of God's name.

76

Hurricane Katrina – Law and Order

The rule of law is almost always taken for granted by those happy enough to have been brought up in a society blessed with it. In the United Kingdom, it is rare for "normal" people to get excited about the concept of the rule of law, any more than they get excited about the sun or the rain – one just assumes that they will always be with us, particularly the rain. We grow up confident that there will always be a mostly impartial and incorruptible police force to turn to in times of trouble and to keep law and order. Having lectured on democratisation in places where the rule of law has never recently existed or has become fractured, I have seen the excitement in the eyes of the young at the thought that they might come to live in a rule of law society. Jewish thought has always value the rule of law, partly because we have been so graphically exposed to the dangers of its absence at different periods of our history. (From 10th September 2005)

The brutal anarchy reported from certain places affected by Hurricane Katrina, particularly in shelters resorted

to by those displaced from their homes, vividly and hor-
rifyingly illustrates the warning of the rabbis in Pirkei
Ovos (3:2) that we should pray for the welfare of the
state machinery because without it each person would
swallow his neighbour alive.

This striking piece of imagery is chosen, says the
gemoro (Avodoh Zoroh 72) to create a picture of
the strong bullying and exploiting the weak in much the
same way as the larger fish in the sea habitually swallow
those smaller than them: without either compassion or
active hostility or dislike, but merely as an instinctive
product of an all-absorbing self-interest.

That instinctive self-interest is entirely natural to the
animal world: and it is entirely natural to man but can
be modified by discipline. One form of discipline is that
imposed by the rule of law, the state machinery in its
widest aspects, for which the rabbis exhort us to pray.

But the rule of law is always fragile: quite how fragile,
we have seen in the reports of behaviour during this
most recent disaster in America. Its effectiveness depends
entirely on the strength of those controlling the law, and
their ability to restrain a partly reluctant population,
many of whom are aware that the forces constraining
them are themselves vulnerable to many greater forces,
both natural and unnatural. When one of those greater
forces intervenes to prevent the enforcement of law and
order, chaos erupts.

For this reason, the Maggid of Kelm stresses that in
this morning's Torah reading the injunction to appoint
judges and policemen (Devorim 16:18) is phrased in the
second person singular, not plural. He therefore reads it
as including a requirement for each person to develop
methods of self-discipline, which will regulate, condition

and train his or her selfish instincts more effectively and permanently than can be achieved by the imposition of outside constraints.

A society that wishes the weak to be protected, and that wishes to see expounded in practice the Torah principles of kindness, sharing and caring, should see the forces of law and order only as a secondary line of recourse; the front line of the enterprise should be the task of educating and encouraging people to discipline themselves in matters of civic and community responsibility.

In England today, citizenship is a compulsory part of the curriculum for secondary school students. If taught imaginatively and creatively it can cause young people to think of themselves and others in an entirely new way. An urgent message of the lawlessness seen in America in the past two weeks is that too many people are being allowed to reach adulthood without acquiring a sufficient sense of citizenship to act as a control on their animal instincts of selfishness once the physical constraints of law and order are relaxed.

Let us as Jews, with a mission inherited from our father Abraham who taught the whole world a concept of kindness based on the monotheist vision of all people as brothers and sisters created by a single God for a single purpose, resolve not merely to pray for the continued power of the forces of law and order but also to do whatever we can to provide an example of responsible citizenship and to encourage others to emulate it.

CHARITIES

77

All Proceeds to Charity – Promise or Prayer?

There is a rabbinic dictum that the Torah should not be turned into "a spade to dig with". The thought is honoured today more in the breach than the observance. In particular, the religious affiliations of the Jewish community are sometimes relied upon to fund charities whose principal business appears to be to provide salaries for chief executives and others that they would find it difficult to command from that portion of the world that cannot be made to believe that it "owes them a living". (From 21st December 2009)

Nowadays it is common to see the words "all proceeds to charity" or something along those lines on all kinds of advertisements, from books to concerts.

There are, however, a few potential ambiguities with this formula, based on the uncertainty of what is meant by "all", what is meant by "proceeds", what is meant by "to" and what is meant by "charity".

Proceeds is generally understood in this context to mean profits, and fair enough: although in some cases the actual cost of producing whatever it is has been generously underwritten by a charitable donor, in which case the gross receipts from "customers" may go to charity, in most cases it is accepted that proceeds means proceeds net of actual expenses.

But what amounts to actual expenses in this context varies widely. In particular, where the person who is offering the service is paying himself or herself a salary out of the charity's funds, "expenses" is likely to include a deduction that goes into the pocket of that person and possibly other employees of the charity.

Again, fair enough, one may say: people who run charities also like to eat occasionally; and where a charity requires more time and expertise than can be provided by a part-time amateur, the charity will of course need to factor into its running expenses the costs of salaries for its staff.

But in order to avoid halachic questions of theft from public funds and g'neivas da'as ("stealing the mind" – creating a false impression), three things are needed – transparency, accountability and proportionality.

As to transparency, it should be clear to donors that they are contributing towards the living expenses of the person or persons running the charity. Sometimes this will be sufficiently clear by implication: but not always – and if there is reasonable ambiguity, it should be dispelled in some appropriately express way. And if the person collecting for charity is on a commission, the amount of that commission should be made clear to the donor at the time of soliciting the donation.

As to accountability, charities should not just produce the accounts required by the Charity Commission: they should produce and publish their complete accounts so that people who donate even small amounts are likely to have access to the accounts. For example, if a charity has a standing advertisement in a synagogue, the annual accounts should be sent to the synagogue and it should be invited to exhibit them in the same way.

As to proportionality, salaries should be proportionate both to the resources of the charity and to the qualifications of the person providing the services. One sometimes suspects that people pay themselves or are paid out of charitable funds salaries at a rate that they would find it hard to command in the commercial sector.

Those who run charities without charging for their time, or who give all their time to charities and charge a reasonable amount for it, do an immense service both to those whom the charity benefits and to all of us who they allow to participate in it through donations. But by agreeing to run a charity one accepts a sacred trust that must not be tainted by hidden or unreasonable personal gain.

78

Money for Nothing?

I love the story below and find it refreshingly heart-warming every time I read it. It is always so good to remind ourselves that gratitude and other excellent human trays are to be found at large if one only looks for them; and it is always salutary to remind oneself that some of the most potent examples Are provided by people who do not regard themselves as religious or spiritual at all, but simply motivated by human instinct. (From 28th May 2009)

A lovely lady has just died and left her former neighbours around the village of Solva a large amount of money, in a wide variety of bequests.

I just heard a radio journalist ask the local publican how he felt about it. He answered, "well when someone gives you money for nothing you're bound to feel good about it".

Thereby missing the point of the bequest. This was not "money for nothing" – it was a celebration of gratitude for real – but intangible – benefits received from the warmth and companionship of the whole village.

This lady has taught us a wonderful lesson in the Jewish principle of *hakoras hatov* – gratitude – one of the key attributes ascribed to the Divine image in which we are all created.

What good timing as well: this lesson comes on the eve of Shavuot, on which festival we read about Ruth, another lady who taught the Jewish community a powerful lesson in the practice of our own Jewish values. Ruth, indeed, did it so effectively that the influx of much-needed spiritual energy that she brought to the community was the foundation for the birth and nurture of King David, from whose descendants the Messiah will eventually come. We are much in need of bursts of constructive spiritual energy today – a few more lessons in gratitude like this one, and we may be ready for King David's successor.

79

Crooked Philanthropy

Why is it that so many people think that if they give back to society some of the money that they have stolen or extorted in the course of their professional or commercial lives, they have done something to be proud of? And why is it that the community appears to fall for it every time, and treats any crook who wishes to endow a synagogue as a saint in the making? (From 18th March 2006)

A man who spent time in prison having been convicted of financial wrong-doing is to provide money and other assistance for a major new communal project. A number of Torah concepts come immediately to mind—

(1)   Mitzvoh haboh ba'aveiroh eino mitzvoh. Robin Hoodism is contrary to the Torah. Money that is acquired wrongly does not become purged by being given to a good cause. Indeed, if I have reason to believe that money has been dishonestly acquired I may not receive it, whether for my own use or for anyone else's.

(2)   Hatovel v'sheretz beyodo. To build a communal institution designed to spread Torah values

using money acquired by their breach is like, in the symbolism of the Talmud, someone who goes to the mikveh while clutching a source of tumoh in his hand. Better not to build than to build with tainted money.

(3)   Teshuvoh. Any criminal can repent and become rehabilitated. But it requires not mere regret and good intentions, but an active attempt to compensate for the harm done. In the case of gezel min horabim – theft from a class not all of whose members can be ascertained – it is very difficult to make any meaningful reparation. But there are ways that one could try. Giving to a parochial and sectarian institution, having caused monetary loss to members of the wider community, is clearly insufficient.

(4)   Ma'aris ho'ayin. We must be seen to act properly, as well as acting properly. The criminal in question may have tried to make effective reparation to the wider community. But unless his attempts are made as public as his involvement in the communal enterprise, the latter will be tainted by the appearance of profiting from the loss caused to the wider public.

(5)   Chillul hashem. Anything which makes it appear that the Jewish community is prepared to honour and to be led by dishonest people brings discredit on the name of God, to glorify which is our only communal responsibility.

80

Charity in the Credit Crunch

Charity has always been key to the Jewish religion and the Jewish community. In times of financial austerity, it becomes even more important to be charitable, of course; and it also becomes increasingly important to make sure that within religious communities in general we bring our children up so far as possible with the skills and inclination to be as self-sufficient as possible, while recognising that all material success is a divine blessing. (From 2nd December 2008)

This Thursday, the Agudah Rabbonim have called a day of prayer on account of the continuing and deepening impact of the recession. With so many local families and institutions in financial difficulty, the rabbis urge us to pray for Divine compassion.

At the same time, they remind us that those of us who are still blessed with jobs and sufficient incomes should be giving what we can to communal institutions and other tzedokohs.

The concept of the tithing of income derives from this week's parashah; at the end of a conversation between Yaakov and Hashem (Bereishis 28:20-22).

Yaakov says to Hashem, in essence, "if you are with me on my journey, give me food and clothing and bring me home safely, then I will give back one tenth of whatever you give me".

A strange way to talk to God. Striking a bargain with God in this peremptory fashion is strange enough to begin with. And to promise to pay the donor for a benefit conferred by agreeing to return one tenth of the benefit is strange enough to be going on with; how should that convince the donor to give?

The practice of tithing is a recognition that everything belongs to and comes from God. If we recognise the Divine origin of everything we have, we can turn to God with confidence and trust, and ask Him to continue His blessings; by promising to use them for good (a concept which includes, but is not limited to, setting a part aside for others) we are trying to make ourselves fitting recipients.

In hard times when we are confronted by financial difficulties on all sides it is that much easier not to take our material blessings for granted; if realising our blessings encourages us to give increasingly generously to various causes, encouraged by the increased importance and potential impact of a small amount of money in troubled times, we can see why the rabbis have always stressed that the perfect Messianic world is more likely to emerge out of troubled times – nothing is more likely to lead to it than an enhanced sense of our responsibilities to each other and the importance of sharing our blessings.

81

Kosher Casinos and the Chinese Auction

Gambling is one of the most dangerous social evils today, destroying families and wrecking lives for the sake of allowing greedy people to exploit the weak and vulnerable. Judaism has always been clear about the contempt in which gamblers are held and the questionable lawfulness of gambling transactions – so why has gambling become a common feature of Jewish charitable fund-raising? (From 14th November 2004)

The Government's recently introduced Gambling Bill has attracted a certain amount of controversy, principally because of the proposals to relax the restrictions on the number and size of casinos.

The Government's policy in relation to gambling is apparent from the fact that the Bill obliges the new Gambling Commission "to permit gambling, in so far as the Commission thinks it reasonably consistent with pursuit of the objectives of—

    (a)   preventing gambling from being a source of crime or disorder, being associated with crime or disorder or being used to support crime,

(b) ensuring that gambling is conducted in a fair and open way, and

(c) protecting children and other vulnerable persons from being harmed or exploited by gambling." (clauses 1 and 21).

One might be excused for thinking that Jewish sources shared the perception that gambling is unobjectionable in itself although requiring to be carried on in such a way as to avoid a number of inherent dangers.

Certainly, the charitable institutions of the Jewish community increasingly take every opportunity to exploit the allure of gambling, and the rabbis do not appear to protest (or at any rate have not so far acted in such a way as to prevent the trend).

Gone are the days of the obviously harmless 10-pence a ticket lottery, with prizes that were so unappealing that they were clearly not designed to act as a serious incentive to parting with money. Now glossy brochures advertising the latest charity's "Chinese Auction" slip through the letter-box every few weeks – and, whether or not the Chinese had anything to do with it, these auctions amount simply to agglomerations of individual lotteries, in which the tickets cost anything from £10 to £100, and the prizes are said to be worth hundreds or thousands. Normally there is also a "split-the-pot" game, which is a straight lottery with an unrestricted cash prize determined only by the number of people wishing to participate.

And apart from these "auctions", the orthodox Jewish press is constantly advertising simple lotteries with enormous prizes – cars, flats, or on one particularly tasteless occasion a Sefer Torah – and correspondingly high costs of tickets.

It is certainly true that there is no halachic prohibition against gambling. But it is equally true that Jewish thought disapproves of gambling so highly as to equate it with a form of theft, on the grounds that each party to a gambling transaction enters into it only on the basis of his belief that he will win. If a person knew for certain that he would not win, he would not bet. Unlike in a genuine commercial transaction, therefore, he does not really intend the other party to acquire his money, but hopes that he will retain his money and acquire someone else's.

On this analysis, not only is gambling at least bordering on the dishonest, but neither is it an attractive or useful pursuit, furthering the welfare of the community. On both these grounds, habitual gamblers are included in the list of wrong-doers disqualified for giving evidence in a beis din.

All this makes one wonder why Jewish charities have anything to do with gambling. In former days, the ready answer was "it isn't really gambling – people are happy to give anyway, and this is just a bit of fun". That was probably mostly or even entirely true of the ten-pence lottery tickets. But it is clearly not true of the high-stake, high-prize lotteries described above. As to these, the prizes are being used as real incentives to encourage people to part with money that they would otherwise either keep themselves or, if using ma'aser money, give to other charities. In the former case, there is a real question of "avak gezel" (near-theft) from the gambler (and therefore a problem of mitzvo habo b'aveiro), while in the latter case there must be a similar issue in relation to the advantage gained over other charities.

One wonders why the rabbis do not intervene. Perhaps they do, or will. But as is so often the case there is no need for the Jewish public to wait for a clear prohibition to be applied or for disastrous social consequences to result in a rabbinic decree.

We should give our own message to charities. While you offer us the opportunity to do a good deed with money that Hashem has given us, we value you as partners in our spiritual growth. But when you seek to mix our motives, and to acquire our money not based on a pure motive of enhancing society but on a sordid mixture containing an element of greed, we will give our money elsewhere.

82

The End does not Justify the Means (2) – Charity Gambling

In my frequent rants against charity fund-raising gambling, the aspect of child exploitation is one that I rarely get worked up about: but I'm not sure why not – the spectacle of children being told to pressurise friends and relations into "sponsoring them" to walk, run or swim – whatever that means – is not endearing. There is always the danger that someone is embarrassed into giving when they didn't really want to, which raises questions for the charity of avak gezel (quasi-theft). And it tends to give children a slightly skewed perspective on the world, to think that their having fun means that I should donate to a charity. The events discussed in this piece manage to combine the use of gambling and the exploitation of children. (From 11th December 2007)

The son of the rabbi of my shul was hawking raffle tickets this morning to collect money for his school (a separatist institution – of which more another posting).

In Jewish thought, there are two kinds of objection to gambling. First, it is close to theft, because the fool who gambles does not really intend to part with his money – at the moment of placing the stake his imagination suspends his reason; if he knew for certain that he was going to lose the stake, he would not put it down. Secondly, money won by gambling is not money earned by contributing to the well-being of the world, but by preying parasitically on the dreams of the weak-minded.

A 50p charity raffle ticket is not serious gambling, by either of these tests. The person giving the money is happy to see it go to a good cause, and is giving it out of charitable intent (or, possibly, embarrassment – but we hope for the best).

A £100 ticket for a chance to win a car, with the number of tickets advertised as inducement to rely on maximum chances of winning, is gambling pure and simple. Whether the money is being collected by a businessman or a charity, the process is contrary to Jewish law and the only difference is that the charity ought certainly to know better.

Between the two extremes lies a vast grey area where it will be difficult or impossible for a charity to know for certain whether a fund-raising activity is contrary to Jewish law or not. But the charity can be sure of this: appeal to people's worse instincts and you may gain more money, but it will be tainted money and will bring no *simen brochoh* (blessing); appeal to people's best instincts and whatever you collect is a source of true blessing for the charity and for its donors.

83

Why aren't Poppies
more Popular?

Inter-faith activity and the development of cultural diversity should be less about artificial occasions where the great and the good make stilted speeches much of which do not stand up to much in the way of theological scrutiny, and more about ordinary people taking advantage of every opportunity to show respect and to share occasions and activities that are, or ought to be, of equal cultural resonance. (From 6th November 2009)

Sensitivity is the key Jewish value. This week's Torah reading finds Abraham – who discovered Judaism – exploring with God how to maximise the opportunities for even the most wicked and greedy of all cultures, the conurbation of Sodom and Gomorrah, to escape total destruction. And it finds him building a religious philosophy based on the concept of welcoming guests and visitors from all corners of the cultural globe, and ministering to the needs of each with a unique sensitivity.

So presumably the orthodox Jewish community will be alert for ways of feeling and showing sensitivity to others. Sensitivity to the feelings of those who fought, or whose families fought, to preserve a malchus shel chessed – a free and democratic society – where every religion and culture could receive respect and could cherish its own culture and values alongside those of its host society? Sensitivity to the grief of those who every year mourn those who lost their lives in the battle for this country's freedom. And sensitivity to the desire of a free nation to mark its feelings of the senselessness and wickedness of the lust and ambition that soaked the fields of Europe twice in the blood of those whose lives should have been dedicated to something better; the blood-soaked fields of the World War One trenches, whose blood-red poppies were gathered as the guns fell silent in spontaneous tribute to those who fell.

The ranks of the orthodox community should be ablaze with poppies between now and Remembrance Day. It is a rare opportunity to share a cultural and non-religious symbol with all those who live around us, men and women of all religions or of no religion. There are still a few days left to buy our poppies and show Abraham's sensitivity to those around us – let's get buying.

84

Bungee Jumping for
Charity – the Jewish View

How many rabbis does it take to work out that jumping off cliffs is generally unwise behaviour? ... (From 1ˢᵗ May 2012)

On 10th June, the Jewish Student Chaplaincy organisation is arranging a charity event in which chaplains and past and present students will jump from a 140ft Bungee Crane.

A parent of present students asked me to comment on whether this is permissible in halochoh. Clearly, it is not.

Searching the internet reveals a commonly-advanced statistic for bungee jumping of a fatality average of 1 in 500,000 jumps. That, of course, is generally compared favourably with driving a certain distance or crossing the road or being struck by lightning.

But the comparisons miss the point for halachic purposes. I am required to guard the life that God has given me and not to expose myself to unnecessary risks, for which purpose "necessary" is determined by reference to whether the risk is reasonably proportionate to the need to undertake the potentially dangerous activity.

Since there is no need to fall off a crane attached to a piece of elastic, the acceptable level of risk in doing so is nil.

"But it's for charity" – this makes no difference. If it would be wrong to do something without the excuse of raising money, it is wrong to do it despite that excuse. Indeed, charities should generally be more careful than they are about profiting only from permitted activities (and not, for example, selling £100 tickets for a chance to win a car, which is gambling of a kind strongly disapproved of in halochoh).

Worse than that, if a charitable motive encourages people to do something that they would have enough sense not to do otherwise, the charity is transgressing the Biblical prohibition of putting a stumbling block before the blind.

Someone who wants to Bungee jump as part of an athletic exercise, or for sight-seeing purposes, and as part of a carefully calculated assessment against the small risk against the great pleasure they expect to feel, they may have a halachic justification. (Whether that would apply to a person with dependent family is, of course, more doubtful.) But in this case people who would otherwise have no wish to jump off a crane, and may actually be frightened in doing so, are being encouraged to conquer their instincts (which some may recognise as common sense) because of the gratitude that they feel for the chaplains.

The Jewish chaplains are uniformly wonderful people whose dedication and service are exemplary.

Their care of our students is superbly inspirational; it should, however, extend to discouraging past and present students (and themselves) from jumping off a crane, which is generally regarded as an unwise thing to do.

85

Haiti – Giving Tzedokoh Funds to Disaster Relief

To those who say that ma'aser money (tithe of income set aside for charitable purposes) cannot be used for giving to disaster relief which solely or primarily benefits non-Jews, the obvious answer is: "fine, so don't give ma'aser money ... but just give...". (From 16th January 2010)

Amidst the appalling disaster and devastation of the Haiti earthquake, it is at least good to know that the reaction of so many people around the world has been "what can we do to help?".

And it is also good to know that the Jewish community is not backward in coming forward. Israel had its team of medics standing by ready to join the relief efforts within hours of the news hitting the media. And Jews around the world are joining others in contributing funds to the relief campaigns.

The issue of using tzedokoh funds for humanitarian disaster relief is rather simple, but I discuss it here because I have received reports of at least one person who should know better – being responsible for children's spiritual development – talking nonsense.

There are two main Talmudic principles involved.

First, the allocation of limited resources is that "the poor of your city come before the poor of other places". That applies at all levels, so my family come first, my local community comes next, and so on outwards.

The rabbis record that we give to non-Jewish charities as well as to Jewish charities because of "darchei sholom" – the ways of peace – and there is considerable discussion as to what precisely this means.

Common sense makes it clear that the first principle does not and could not mean "do not give a penny to another city until your city has everything it could possibly wish for", because on that basis nobody would ever get beyond their own immediate family in giving tzedokoh. What it does mean is that in deciding how to divide whatever I am giving to charitable purposes overall, I give relatively more to those for whom I am more responsible by virtue of proximity and expectation, and less to those for whom I am less responsible.

As to the second principle, what is required by darchei sholom has changed in the last few decades in a number of ways. When we lived in small isolated villages in Poland, our responsibilities were limited by our knowledge. Famines in Africa were thought of, if at all, as remote events affecting people of whom we knew little or nothing. Nowadays, almost every Jew in this country sees the world news in a newspaper of some kind or on the television or hears it on the radio. Almost every Jew will at some point last week have seen the faces of people wounded by the earthquake, and most will have heard their cries.

Whether one sees the principle of *darchei sholom* as being primarily about our community's international reputation or about our own self-respect and spiritual direction, it is simply impossible that the descendants of our father Abraham could see the faces of the injured and hear the cries of the suffering and not be moved to wish – almost to need – to be associated in some small way in the efforts to relieve their suffering.

And we can rest assured that when we give money to the disaster relief funds we are following the example of sensitivity set by the gedolei Torah over the years – the "Tzaddik in Our Time" Reb Aryeh Levine, for example, gave money to African famine relief: although immersed in the Old City with very limited opportunity for finding out about events in the wider world, the cries of the famine-stricken somehow found their way to his ears with the inevitable result.

Put another way, the application of the principles of "your city first" and "*darchei sholom*" has been affected by the shrinking of the world: my brother in Africa is no longer a remote concept, it is an actual face that I have seen. Individuals will make their own decisions about the allocation of their own resources. Some may prefer not to give their basic ma'aser tithes to humanitarian disasters of this kind, but to add to their ma'aser money for this purpose. Whatever each person's individual decision, we can feel closest to our father Abraham at moments like this when we are following his lead in serving God by caring for mankind.

GENERAL SOCIETY ISSUES

86

Rabbi Dweck, Rabbi Bassous and Homosexuality

As if we weren't already a sufficiently divided commu-
nity as well as one that tends to concentrate on the ines-
sential, a recent issue about what Jewish leaders can and
cannot say to help the gay community feel comfortable
within Judaism has been turned almost entirely into a
political power struggle within the rabbinic community.
(From 25th June 2017)

Rabbi Dweck is an enormously charismatic personality
and he clearly cares very deeply about the Jewish community, particularly those who are finding it increasingly hard to straddle the two worlds of orthodox
Judaism and the modern secular world. He got a bit
carried away at one point in a shiur when he used
certain phrases, which he has since publicly modified
or retracted. And personally, I think he is suggesting
detaching a particular biblical prohibition from other
aspects of an accompanying lifestyle in a way that runs
contrary to the traditional halachic approach of surrounding prohibitions with fences, the laws of yichud

being perhaps the most relevant example in this general area.

Rabbi Bassous is one of the rabbis who has given a public lecture denouncing Rabbi Dweck – I listened to his lecture on YouTube and personally I found the tone much more repellent than the tone of anything that Rabbi Dweck said; it seemed to me to be a piece of rabble-rousing in the best traditions of religious bigotry and intolerance, and did nothing to help heal wounds or advance understanding.

Most of the reaction to Rabbi Dweck has been to play the man and not the ball: rather than focusing on the subject of homosexuality, the controversy has turned into a general tirade against his general approach. (He is, as I say, burdened with enormous charm and charisma, both serious handicaps for a religious leader that make it very difficult to avoid saying the occasional daft thing – and which inevitably attract the envy of less effective leaders.)

Homosexuality and other gender issues are among the most pressing issues confronting young Jews today. The modern world is readjusting at such an enormous pace that it is becoming very difficult to keep up. Much of halachah is necessarily reflective of culture, and the faster culture is changing around us the more difficult it is to work out what parts of halachah can and must develop to remain reflective of and relevant to the modern world, for those of us who choose to live in it and not to hide from it.

Unless religious leaders openly and regularly confront the substance of gender issues, the Jewish orthodox community will necessarily be left behind by the pace of change, and a generation of young Jews risks being alienated, excluded and lost.

I don't know exactly where we should end up on all this. Ideally, we would deal with much of the problem by a combination of tolerance and sensitivity on everybody's part. If a young male couple come to my shul every week, are known to live together, and address each other affectionately, there is no reason why they should not feel as fully welcomed as part of the community as anyone else, and as fully involved in the community's religious and social activities: as Rabbi Dweck says, none of their behaviour involves a prohibition, and I don't need to make any assumptions about what they do in their own home and I don't need to start any witch-hunts. If they come in wearing gay-pride tee-shirts and demand the right to give a shiur about sexual equality and the barbaric nature of certain biblical prohibitions, I will need to explain that I cannot accommodate them within an orthodox Jewish community. And hopefully whatever we do will be done sensitively and in a way that expresses love of humanity rather than smug self-appreciation of our own supposed holiness.

So, discretion and tolerance could get us a long way: but I fear things may have got beyond the point at which either "side" will be content with that.

87

How Can Politicians Regain Public Trust?

Ironically, I wrote this piece about two years before the main MPs' expenses scandal broke, as a result of which public trust in MPs took another drastic turn for the worse. It is striking to think that a contemporary challenge of political life has apparently been considered by communal and political leaders for many generations. Getting the balance right between ensuring that people without independent means are able to take part in public life and preventing exploitation of public positions is as tricky now as it was in the time of Moses: but, as in those days and as this piece shows, if it is generally necessary to err in one direction or another at the margins, there can be no doubt as to which direction of error is to be preferred. (From 15th December 2007)

Politicians from all parties have commented recently on what they see as an increasing problem of lack of trust on the part of the public in politics and politicians generally. While their perceived reasons vary, all point to the fact that the public feel that at some time and in some way, they have been misled by politicians.

When Joseph's brothers told their father Jacob that Joseph was alive, his heart missed a beat because he didn't believe them (Bereishis 45:26). But according to the rabbis Jacob had always known that Joseph was alive (Rashi on Bereishis 37:25): so why did he find it difficult when the brothers confirmed that Joseph was alive? The answer is simply this: the brothers had lied to Jacob – and when a confirmed liar tells me the truth, it is more likely to make me doubt the truth than to believe the liar. Because the brothers told him that Joseph was alive, for the first time Jacob wondered whether perhaps he was dead.

So how did the brothers regain Jacob's trust? The verse in Bereishis 45:26 says they adopted two strategies: (a) they made sure that they told Jacob everything that Joseph had said to them, irrespective of whether or not it reflected well on the brothers, and (b) they made sure that Jacob saw the solid evidence of Joseph's health and influence, the gifts he had sent. Jacob was quickly satisfied.

If politicians are right that there is a need to regain public trust, they can also adopt these two strategies. Actions speak louder than words, and the public only need to be shown unimpeachable, solid evidence of the performance of promises to regain trust very fast. And if people feel they are being told both the good and the bad, they will be prepared to believe both; if they feel they are being told only the good and not the bad, they will believe neither.

88

Nobel Games and Noble Aspirations

There is no limit to the ability of science to facilitate and inform all areas of human endeavour. And there is therefore no end to the needs to remind scientists that invaluable as they and their knowledge are, they need to keep their pronouncements strictly and scientifically within the area of their own professional expertise. It is only politicians and rabbis who are allowed to pretend to know everything about everything: and we permit them that pretence because it rests on the silence truth that in reality they know very little about anything. Since we look up to scientists in their own field and rely on them implicitly, it is all the more important that they each stick to their own field and resist the natural human temptation to Expand their horizons of their perceived infallibility. (From 15th October 2005)

Professor Robert Aumann deserves warm congratulations from the world-wide Jewish community, not least for the wonderful kiddush hashem created by the international media coverage of his smile beaming out from under his kippah.

That apart, like other practical social sciences applied games theory clearly has enormous benefits for society in all kinds of ways.

Also like other sciences, it is important to understand its limitations, which Professor Aumann clearly does. In particular, asked about the application of games theory to the Israel-Palestine conflict, he is reported as having said "It's been going on for more than 80 years and … it's going to go on for at least another 80. I don't see any end to it."

Without knowing the precise context of the question to which these remarks responded, it is impossible to be sure exactly what Professor Aumann meant. But knowing him to be a Torah Jew we can be sure what he did not mean: he may have meant that his particular science has nothing to offer for the acceleration of the resolution of conflict in Israel, but he certainly did not mean that there is therefore no hope for peace.

Professor Aumann himself has witnessed miracles: a miraculous escape from the inferno and a miraculous rebuilding, in other lands in general and in Israel in particular, of so much of what was lost. Therefore, he is better-placed than many to know that the cry of the believing Jew through the ages when confronted with the limits of science and human endeavour is not the cry of despair but the cry of hope beyond reason but within faith.

Standing at the brink of the sea with the Egyptian armies massing behind them, Moses turns to the Jewish people and says not "my political, diplomatic and military strategies have reached the end of their potential and we may as well give up" but rather "my political, diplomatic and military strategies have come to the limit of their potential and we can therefore, all human effort having been expended and failed, confidently expect immediate divine intervention" (see Shemos 14:13-14).

We are all deeply indebted to Professor Aumann and all other scientists, social and other, for their discoveries that enable us to work faster and more effectively towards the goal of a perfect world under the Kingship of God. But we never forget that the human effort can only succeed in accordance with the God's blessings, and that ultimate success, personally, communally and universally, owes more to faith in God's mercies and kindness than to our own efforts. And so, the more impossible the task that we confront seems, the more confidently we trust in God to achieve it for us once we have deserved it.

89

Crises and Conscience – Preparing for Choices

Although it is perhaps not the worst thing in the world that a typical orthodox kiddush (religious meal) at the end of a Saturday morning service resembles nothing as much as feeding time at the zoo, it is extremely troubling that people appear not to mind that has come to be expected of these occasions, and they seem to find it a source of amusement and even a warped kind of pride. A non-Jewish colleague of my wife's who attended a kiddush once saw everybody scrabbling at the tables to help themselves, so he commandeered a tray of biscuits and started offering it to people who have not yet battled their way to the table: on approaching one regular worshipper he was treated to a condescending grin and the comment "I guess you're not Jewish then!" Similarly, many people appear to find nothing incongruous about pushing one's way through the queue at the bakers to grab food to take home to put on the Sabbath table over which psalms invoking peace for humanity will doubtless be intoned. Perhaps natural and perhaps partly harmless: but, as I say below: "if I push through *a bus queue today, I am more likely to push through a lifeboat queue tomorrow; if I think about decency while waiting for the bus, I increase my chances of behaving decently while waiting for a lifeboat." Rather well put, I thought. (From 15th January 2012)*

A number of survivors from the Costa Concordia either woke up, or should have woken up, with slightly troubled consciences this morning.

According to survivors, attempts to prioritise women, children and the infirm in boarding the lifeboats were obstructed by able-bodied men insisting on remaining with their families.

Those who succeeded in forcing their way into lifeboats may never know whether, or to what extent, they were responsible for others' trauma, injuries or even possibly death.

Perhaps they won't think about it or care; or perhaps they will justify their actions to themselves.

And it is, of course, easier for me to hope and imagine that I would have behaved better in the same circumstances, than to be sure of it; as the Ethics of the Fathers (Pirkei Avot) say, don't judge someone until you stand in his or her place (which is of course impossible).

But thinking about all this does remind me of what I believe to be a central purpose of religion; to learn how to control myself in trivial ways and at unimportant moments so that I will be able to display self-control in significant ways and at times of crisis.

The Chofetz Chaim said that no choice in life is difficult to make – but it is often very difficult to know when I am making a choice, or what choice I am making. To analyse my own behaviour, and the options open to me, carefully and critically at a time of crisis requires a habit of self-examination and self-discipline.

People who behave like animals at the best of times are unlikely suddenly to discover human decency at the worst of times.

People who, through religion or in other ways, aim during "normal" times to rise above the purely animal instincts and to direct their behaviour through self-control and thought for others, have at least a chance of being able to behave decently under pressure.

If I push through a bus-queue today, I am more likely to push through a life-boat queue tomorrow; if I think about decency while waiting for the bus, I increase my chances of behaving decently while waiting for a life-boat.

That may not affect my success in life – many people who behave like the worst kind of animal appear to achieve the best kind of material success; but I believe that it will affect my chances of nurturing inside me something that is not too closely bound to the purely material world to live on after my physical death.

90

Respect

The idea that "derech eretz kadma laTorah" (manners come before Torah) is a common aphorism oft-repeated within orthodox Jewish circles; but it is honoured more in the breach than the observance ... (From 28th April 2006)

It is a recurring current theme of politicians and social commentators that modern Britain is seriously deficient in the matter of respect. So much so that "respect" is increasingly used as a political tag designed to attract automatic approval and has in at least one case been incorporated into the title of a political movement. But while everyone can agree that respect, like apple pie and motherhood, is a good thing, unlike apple pie and motherhood it is difficult or impossible to define what is meant by respect; and one suspects that it means very different things to different people, and is often used as a conveniently empty label to attach to a person's individual desiderata.

The Torah is very strong on manners generally. The rabbis even ventured the radical Talmudic assertion derech eretz kodmo laTorah which can be roughly rendered into English as good behaviour precedes, and is a prerequisite of, Torah observance. Radical, because it appears to suggest not merely that good behaviour between humans is a crucial part of the Torah – a concept with which we are all familiar – but that good behaviour is a value which exists outside and independent of the Torah. Which would be radical indeed, and even blasphemous, were it not for the other rabbinic assertion histakel b'oraisoh u'boro olmo – that God looked into the Torah and created the world. In other words, the world was created to reflect and implement Torah values, rather than the Torah being created to make sense of the world. Derech eretz kodmo laTorah is therefore an assertion that the requirements of derech eretz belong in some ineffable way to that part of the Torah which exists independently of the world, and is not merely a terrestrial detail provided to further implementation of the underlying Torah values.

The Torah does not offer us anywhere a compendious definition of derech eretz. But it does offer sufficient instances and examples for us to be able to construct a workable set of guidelines.

One example occurs in this week's parashah. A person who finds that he has a tzora'as patch on the walls of his or her house, is required to send for a Cohen to pronounce whether it is or is not actually tzora'as. And the Torah prescribes the words to be used in asking the Cohen – "k'nega niro li baboyis" ("there is something on my house that appears to me like nega tzora'as") (Vayikro 14:35). Rashi brings the Talmudic explanation that the owner of the house may be more of an expert than the Cohen in the appearance of tzora'as – but nevertheless out of derech eretz he or she is to say to the Cohen no more than "I think I may have a problem – what do you think?". The Cohen may have to ask the house owner for expert guidance on the matter, but in this way the decencies are preserved and the separate roles of each, Cohen and expert, are acknowledged.

And that is a major key to a practical meaning of respect, although doubtless there are other important facets of it too. Respect is, at least in part, about acknowledging other peoples' roles, and not trying to usurp them. The Pirkei Ovos remind us that everyone has a unique task to perform, even if not everybody's hour has yet arrived, so to speak. The Chofetz Chayim reminds us that in asking for peace we mention the peace of the heavens (oseh sholom bimromov ...) not because the heavens are a field of inactivity but because each celestial body appears to know and rigidly stick to its allotted path, even if it passes within inches of another's.

There is much wrong with today's society, and also much right. Those who are continually searching for ways of improving the nation's general well-being are certainly right to emphasise the importance of respect in so far as it amounts to an appreciation by each person of everybody else's unique roles: each person should recognise his or her own limitations as well as his or her own abilities, so that we can draw on others' potentials to reflect our own limitations.

91

The End of the World may – or may not – be Nigh

As I say in other pieces, Jewish thought has always valued environmental conservation; but for us the ecology is not an end in itself but a means towards the completion of more important aims. In itself, it doesn't matter very much whether the world continues to exist; but while it presents opportunities for self-improvement we are bound to preserve it for that reason. (From 24th October 2004)

A common objective of environmental campaigns is sustainability. That is to say, a test frequently applied in determining the propriety of a use of natural resources is whether it is sustainable itself (as in the case of forestation and irrigation) or whether it threatens the sustainability of all or part of the ecological system (as in the case of the emission of greenhouse gases or the hunting of a species). However, this assumes either that the world ought to be allowed to last forever or, at least, that it is improper for us to do anything that threatens to shorten its likely span of existence.

Jewish thinking has traditionally neither expected nor desired this world to last forever.

Midrashic tradition posits this world as the seventh in a series (based on the number of words in the first verse of the Bible), each of the first six of which was destroyed (based on the rabbinic understanding of the word "sohu" as not meaning "null", as sometimes translated, but as referring to desolate destruction) (incidentally providing one of the many possible rabbinic explanations of dinosaur fossils).

Each world, according to this tradition, is a time-limited experiment created by God to produce some kind of spiritual force, of the nature of which we can comprehend only a very shadowy picture. In the case of this world, the rabbinic construction of the behaviour of Adam ("Adam sinned for the sake of Heaven") suggests the creation of a world in which man descended from an angelic state, in which he obeys God as an automaton without choice, to a state of tension between a selfish animalism and an altruistic holiness. When human altruism finally triumphs over bestial selfishness through an exertion of free will, the product is a kiddush hashem of unequalled proportions, justifying the creation of the world and rendering its continued existence, at any rate in this form, unnecessary.

Hence the difference between the Messianic Era and the World to Come. The former is still "business as usual" so far as nature is concerned (at least according to Maimonides – others differ to a greater or lesser extent) while the latter is the end of this world as we know it. This is why the description "the world to come" is used to describe the state attained by those who die now, as well as the state attained by everyone as a culmination of the perfection of the natural order known as the Messianic Era.

For the Jew, therefore, the continuation of this world is not, in itself, an aim at all. For me personally, I aim at the attainment of a state of wholly spiritual existence after death known as my personal world to come. For the world, I aim to participate in producing an environment which proclaims the existence and kingship of Hashem. With this in mind, the rabbis have often predicted different periods for the life of this world. A number are discussed in Gemara Sanhedrin 97. One that focuses our minds is that of 6,000 years, which on the basis of our traditional numbering would give the world a little over two centuries to go.

Nor does that necessarily seem unreasonable to the modern mind. The world seems tired. Its resources, whatever environmental decisions are taken, will become more than a little stretched in the next couple of hundred years even if the human family increases at a slower rate than at present. And, of course, increasingly sophisticated techniques of astronomical observation have made it possible in recent years for scientists to observe the number of near misses that the world has had in the matter of meteoric collisions and to speculate how long it will be before we sustain a direct hit.

Although much of Jewish law tells us to respect the world and its resources and to use them with care, the prospect of using them solely in order to achieve perpetual sustainability is not one which commends itself. For one thing, we have always believed in the precariousness of the world's existence, and the constant reliance on Hashem's chessed in keeping us alive, which scientists are now beginning to conclude for themselves.

For another, it has always seemed to us to be more important to ensure that we arrive at the next world in a fit spiritual state than that we prolong this world, or our miniscule share in it, to a particular length.

92

Savile and Secularism

The modern rise in the cult of personality has coincided with the rise in technological ways of discovering and exposing people's faults. It seems that just as one decides that a particular politician, pop star or other public figure is actually okay, they turn out to have been having an affair, or have fiddled their tax, or done something else that even in today's imbalanced world topples them from their pedestal. Which all tends to show the importance of giving our children at least a few eternal truths – whether or not based on religion – which will serve as fixed points in their lives and do not depend on anyone else's transient image. (From 14th October 2012)

The sudden reversal of the public image of Jimmy Savile reminds me of one of the few strong points that institutional religions still have going for them.

Children raised in any environment, religious or secular, will look around for role models, because human beings are naturally imitative and inspiration is a human need.

In an environment that does not subscribe to religion or another all-encompassing philosophy, there is no choice but to seek inspiration in individuals. Many children, and adults, are left with nothing to look up to but the public images of footballers or singers, even though they can inspire people to nothing more than the acquisition of wealth and obsession with self-gratification, neither of which are particularly helpful life-goals.

How often must Savile have been held up as a particularly inspiring role model, since his celebrity was so largely earned by and directed to the doing of purely secularly-inspired good deeds, from volunteering as a hospital porter to realising the dreams of those in distress? But in the space of a few days, the inspirational value of his life is reduced to less than nothing, recalling Undy Scott's dismissive summary of a fellow corrupt politician in Trollope's *The Three Clerks*: "Yesterday he was a god; to-day he is a devil; to-morrow he'll be a man again; that's all."

In CS Lewis' *That Hideous Strength*, a young woman raised in a vehemently anti-religious environment turns to a fellow member of a resistance movement who has dared to doubt the wisdom of its leader and asks him indignantly whether there is no such thing as loyalty. Her colleague, a staunch atheist product of a religious background, turns to her with "generations of Calvinists glinting in his eyes" (I cannot find the book just now, but the actual quote is much better than that!) and remarks something along the lines of "Young lady, indeed there is, and as you grow older you will find that it is too precious a commodity to lavish on individual personalities".

Organised religion is not without its problems; indeed, sometimes it seems to me to have little but problems left. But it has one immeasurably important advantage: take away the rabbi, priest, imam or other leader who has been preaching the religion, expose him or her as a hypocrite, and the religion remains. Catholicism has been damaged by the revelations of priestly misbehaviour; but it has not been destroyed, because there is more to it than belief in individual personalities. If one exponent of the religion is revealed as a shallow fraud, one can always look for another whose life is enriched by his or her religious conviction; and human frailty and dignity being what they are, one will always find both.

As I bored my children by repeating, with very few exceptions indeed nobody is quite as good or quite as bad as they appear to the outside world. Children who grow up without being offered anything other than individuals to look up to are being condemned to a life of inevitable disappointment.

93

"There is risk in life... just be sensible"? – a Jewish View of the Grand National

Sport has always been an alternative religion in England – and one of the strongest aspects of the parallel is that both are easily turned into excuses for behaviour that would otherwise be considered reprehensible or unwise. (From 15th April 2012)

According to the winning Grand National trainer Paul Nicholls, despite consecutive races in each of which two horses have suffered injuries as a result of which they have been put down, the show should go on. He said to BBC Sport: "There is always risk in sport. A lot of people have to grow up, and realise that it is life. ... We've got to be realistic about this. The horses have the best of everything they could have. They probably have better health care than we have. ... If people are going to continue to participate in sport, there is going to be both a human and animal risk."

There are two obvious fallacies here on which Judaism has a strong and clear message, based on three principles.

Principle one: there is a Biblical requirement to take reasonable care of my own life and health.

Principle two: there is a Biblical requirement to take as much care of other people's life as of my own.

Principle three: animals are entitled to the same consideration, being God's creatures; and it is forbidden to cause them unnecessary suffering.

Sport is not forbidden in Jewish law even if it entails risk: as Nicholls rightly says, there is risk in life, and the Biblical command to take care is to take reasonable care in the context of pursuing a full life, of which exercise and sport are part. But I can assess for myself how much risk is appropriate and reasonable, and make an informed choice whether or not to participate. Horses cannot. So, Fallacy number one: "people have to realise that it is life" – it is acceptable for me to decide for myself what is a reasonable risk, but it is not acceptable for me to decide for an animal that it should be exposed to serious risk of injury and pain, for the gratification of my own or other humans' wish for excitement.

"The horses have the best of everything they could have." Fallacy number two: chessed – kindness – does not create ownership or obligation. If I look after horses nicely, that is my choice not theirs; even if they were capable of feeling gratitude, I do not have the right to assume gratitude and to transfer it into a willingness to repay an assumed obligation by suffering pain and injury to gratify me.

Sport is sometimes described as being something of a religion to some people; there is certainly one clear point of analogy here, the need to guard against the temptation to excuse something that is clearly wrong on the grounds of a broader purpose.

94

Slumdog Millionaire – "It's all a muddle"

Religious leaders have always enjoyed trying to explain the inexplicable. Would black slavery have become unlawful earlier if fewer clerics had sought to justify it in "Heaven fits the back to the burden" terms? And the smug self-satisfied "If we only knew more about the Divine plan ..." is at best a fatuous abnegation of responsibility to think, and at worst a way of justifying the worst of human behaviour. Better to admit that very little in the world makes any sense, and then get on with doing whatever we can to sort out the muddle. (From 3rd February 2009)

I saw the film *Slumdog Millionaire* this week. I came away with two enduring impressions.

First, unease at how much explicit violence and brutality is thought necessary to maintain the interest of a cinema audience today. Going to the cinema only rarely, it is easier to track the changes. Psychologists argue whether on-screen violence has any effect on real behaviour. The rest of us simply know as a matter of common-sense that of course it does. Desensitise people by exposure to graphic violence on screen, and you numb the sensitivities that preserve the Divine image in which each of us was created.

Secondly, the film portrays misery and exploitation on every side. The happy ending is a sugar coating added to the pill as an after-thought, and it is the only implausible part of the film. The rest, the inescapable wretchedness of millions of people's lives, is entirely plausible.

None of this is new, of course. Dickens was portraying the lives of youngsters trapped into crime, prostitution, poverty and beggary many decades ago – and even he was merely continuing an ancient tradition of reporting though fiction what has been a timeless theme of reality. One of Dickens' characters sums the whole thing up for us remarkably well, in a manner that has rarely been surpassed for accuracy and simplicity – Stephen Blackpool's oft-repeated exclamation of ultimate hopelessness "It's all a muddle". A world in which the only people who seem to have the power to control their own and others' destinies inevitably misuse and abuse that power, while for everyone else the world is a board-game on which they are the pieces, moved about at the apparently pointless whim of human and God alike.

In this week's Torah reading B'shalach, the Torah explains that God could have taken the Jews out of Egypt by a short route, but He chose the longer one because He was concerned that if the Jews saw battle with the Plishtim they would return to Egypt. Baffling on many counts. (1) If God wants the Plishtim not to attack, He could arrange for that. (2) And if the Plishtim do attack and God wants the Jews to win, He could see to that just as he sees to victory over the Egyptians for them. (3) If God wants to stop the Jews returning to Egypt He again has a number of options – but given the manner of their leaving and their probable reception, return was probably not high on their list of survival strategies.

There is the usual range of ways of understanding all this. But to some extent, God has already explained what is going in when He told Moses in last week's parashah that the exodus was being stage-managed for the purpose of creating the greatest possible impression of God's powers on the world as a whole, for all time. The Jews are pawns in the game, and the game requires them to be set against the Egyptians and not against the Plishtim. The danger of returning to Egypt is not a danger of actual return, but a danger of returning to the spiritual mentality of the Egyptian culture: the aim of setting the Jews against the Egyptians is to enable the former to rise to the challenge of representing the cultural antithesis of the latter, a people of trust in God and of kindness to each other set against a people of trust only in human strength as epitomised by the successful exploitation of others' weakness.

We are all pawns in God's game, and sooner or later we all come to realise it. Even the exploiters reach a stage in their lives when they realise that their battle to control events is finally over, and that only God knows what comes next.

But there are two ways to be a pawn. One can recognise it from the beginning and submit, realising that it is only the choices that are left to me that matter, and that instead of struggling to expand the boundaries of my own power to control events around me I should concentrate on making the right decisions in relation to matters that appear to be "delegated" to me. Or one can resent the external control and struggle constantly against it, the futility of the exercise being masked by apparent successes from time to time when what God and I want to happen coincide.

Much of this week's parashah is about the Jews' struggle to understand the right way to be a pawn. And it is difficult: because sometimes the Torah tells me to submit – "God will fight for you, and you should just stay quiet" (Shemos 14:14); and at other times the Torah appears to encourage us to set ourselves targets of a physical kind and not just to rely on God to do the work for us. Getting the balance right is an eternal Jewish preoccupation. But although we will never be satisfied that we have got the balance quite right, at least we understand the aim of the exercise.

I will never understand why some people are born in an Indian slum to a life of poverty, easy prey for all kinds of miserable exploitation; any more than I will ever understand why I was not. We are all pawns in God's game, and nobody asks me to understand it, or even to like it. All I can do is to submit to what I cannot change, and to concentrate on making good choices where I appear to be given the ability to change anything. Sometimes my path in the game will come so close to someone else's that I have the ability to make theirs easier for them: when that happens, I get pleasure from my apparent ability to help them, although in reality the help comes from God who put Pawn A into the path of Pawn B at the right time. So long as I don't take my own part in it too seriously, no harm is done.

95

Happy Big Bang Day

I've never found it easy to understand why people find apparent tension between science and religion; and I am reliably informed that this is because I understand nothing about science and little about religion. But all the discussions that I have seen appear to end up somewhere very near the rather simple proposition in this piece, that science is knowledge about the how, and religion is belief about the why. (From 10th September 2008)

It is very exciting that scientists have managed today to begin a challenging and long-awaited experiment into the nature of matter. Here are a few random thoughts generated in my mind by this morning's launch of the protons.

First, it is worth saying again that there is no conflict between religious belief and scientific experiment. Indeed, the reverse is the case. The psalmist urges us to consider the magnitude and wonder of God's work of creation, something that we can do more and more effectively the more science reveals to us about it. The Chofetz Chayim explains that the more we appreciate the nature of the creation, the more we can perceive the magnitude of its intended purpose. The founder of our religion, Abraham, came to his revolutionary belief in a single God by examining the nature of the universe, albeit that he had only his own senses to use to conduct the examination.

Secondly, there appears to be a possibility that when this morning's experiment is continued to the collision phase the resultant explosion will destroy the world. Mildly troubling, but much less so to a religious person than to a secular scientist. The rabbis advise us to live each day and each moment as if it were our last – because it always may be. Easier said than done, of course: but at any rate the addition of one more possible reason why my life may end at any moment adds little or nothing to the importance of aiming to be ready at all times to give an account of my life.

Thirdly, the experiment demonstrates both the futility and the value of science. Scientists hoping to be given the meaning of life by colliding a couple of protons are likely to be disappointed: nothing that science has yet achieved (evolutionary theories included) has been successful in discovering, nor is there reason to expect that it will be successful about discovering, anything about the "why" of the world as distinct from the "how". A search for the "why" by flailing about in the universe perpetrating random acts of molecular violence is likely to be futile. But application of increased knowledge of the "how" (evolutionary theories included) to advance our understanding of how we can develop and improve the world, in a partnership with God, to the welfare and benefit of everyone in it, is always of the utmost value from a religious perspective.

96

Smacking Children –
a Jewish Approach

Corporal punishment has often been part of Jewish religious culture; but our religious culture (as distinct from our religious precepts) are necessarily culturally sensitive and vary according to the values of our host nations. Modern sympathies in secular Britain appear to be strongly opposed to corporal punishment, and our religious culture should reflect that. Apart from anything else, a child who does not regard being beaten as unreasonable where that is the prevailing custom, is like to resent it dangerously when he or she knows that it is frowned upon in wider society. (From 21ˢᵗ August 2008)

A few days ago, considerable attention was given by the British media to the case of a father who, angry at his daughter's unruly behaviour towards neighbours, slapped her face in an attempt to shock her out of her ways. The daughter complained to the police, who cautioned the father.

The Jewish attitude to corporal punishment is often summarised by reference to the verse in Proverbs (13:24)

"He who spares his stick hates {often translated as 'spoils'} his son". The implication is that failure to discipline children is not in their interests.

Of course, some explain this verse as purely metaphorical, referring to the concept of discipline in general and not specifically or exclusively to physical punishment.

Clearly, it is open to people to interpret the verse literally or metaphorically. But even those who interpret it literally ought to be aware that, read in a slightly different, but still literal way, it can be seen as imposing an important constraint on those who believe in the importance of physical punishment.

Read the verse in the following way (which classical construction of Biblical Hebrew readily permits): "Who is it who must spare his stick? One who hates his son". It then comes to remind us that corporal punishment should be administered neither in hot blood – at a time when one feels animus against the child of a kind that might cause one to hit out either in the wrong way or for the wrong motive – nor in too cold blood (i.e. so long after the incident as not to appear to the child to be reasonably connected to the incident).

What worried me about the reported incident was the suggestion that the punishment had been a slap around the face delivered in anger. It is never right to hit a child when angry, nor in my opinion is a slap around the face an appropriate form of corporal punishment. Discipline must be delivered when the parent is calm and in control, and in a form which is effective but dignified both for the parent and for the child. The purpose of corporal punishment should not be to relieve a parent's feelings, nor to cause the maximum pain: in my experience when effective at all – and it is not effective or appropriate with all children or for all purposes – it is unnecessary to cause real pain, and the smacking is a purely formal – but sometimes extremely effective – operation.

It is certainly true that failure to discipline one's children effectively does them real harm and amounts to a failure to exercise the responsibilities of a parent: but as always, there are right ways and wrong ways.

97

The Arms Trade

One of the most uncomfortable lessons of international diplomacy is that the United Kingdom government, and other governments world-wide, are frequently in the position of condemning aggression with one hand and supplying the arms to support it with the other. The Torah has some views ... (From 22nd January 2006)

The present discussions about Iran's nuclear ambitions are just the latest aspect of a continuous stream of international tension over the development of particular military technologies. There is a generally shared international concern about the proliferation of weapons of various kinds, including chemical, biological and nuclear technology. But one factor that complicates that concern is the fact that every developed country profits considerably by providing other countries, and particularly less developed countries, with weapons and military equipment of every kind. The international arms trade is so vibrant and profitable that it may appear to the politicians of many countries that they have as much to lose economically by its reduction as they have to gain in other terms. That may be less true of nuclear weaponry, where the potential losses are so cataclysmic, but it is certainly true of conventional weaponry.

With this in mind, a few thoughts about the Torah view of the international arms trade. It is clear halochoh that it is forbidden to sell weapons of any description to anyone who is likely to use them to attack others. It is irrelevant for this purpose whether the assailants, or their potential victims, are Jewish or non-Jewish. The halochoh is of universal application in both respects.

The prohibition extends beyond the sale of actual weaponry, and is expressly applied to the sale of articles designed to be used in warfare for the restraint of prisoners or other purposes, to the sale of raw materials which are exclusively suitable for military purposes, to the provision of services in repairing or improving weapons and to the provision of expert advice in relation to munitions.

There are only three classes of exception or qualification to this very general prohibition.

First, there is a generally (although not universally) accepted exception in the case of articles which are exclusively of defensive use; and the exception may include articles which are primarily defensive but which could be used, perhaps in a last resort, also for aggression.

Secondly, the prohibition on the sale of materials applies only to those relatively few instances of materials that are exclusively applied to military purposes: so, for example, the Gemoro concludes that to sell ordinary metals to people who might use them for military purposes is permissible, but to sell a kind of Indian iron that is in practice acquired exclusively for military purposes is forbidden. As to the sale of multi-purpose raw materials in circumstances that suggest a military purpose behind the purchase, this will be a question of fact and degree.

Thirdly, it is expressly permitted to supply weaponry to an actual or potential protector. As is so often the case, one can more easily isolate these relatively simple halachic principles than one can apply them with certainty to any case. For the present, a few thoughts at a general level—

(1) It can be difficult to determine whether something is primarily aggressive or primarily defensive.

(2) For example, the United Kingdom possesses what it describes as a nuclear deterrent. The deterrent is composed of munitions which are designed entirely for aggressive purposes. But the argument for describing them as a defence is that there is no actual defence against a nuclear attack, except for the deterrent effect produced by a potential aggressor's knowledge that a potential victim has the capability of a nuclear response.

(3) To take another example, anti-aircraft weaponry might legitimately be sold to a sovereign state on the grounds that in normal military circumstances it is exclusively a defence. But to sell the same item to mercenaries who do not have a legitimate defence-role in respect of any territory would enable them, and would seem likely to be intended to enable them, to commit an act of aggression in someone else's territory.

(4)   The sale of materials that are particularly suitable for nuclear research or development would not come under the prohibition where there is a reasonable likelihood of their being intended for use in relation to nuclear power for civil purposes.

(5)   The role of actual or potential protector is necessarily a vague one. The Rabbis suggest that the existence of a formal covenant of protection is significant in this respect. Today, NATO would be an example of a group of nations who have entered into a formal defensive alliance and who thereby become entitled to supply each other with munitions and other military equipment, provided that it is of a kind and in a quantity which is consistent with use for the common defence. And the United Nations appears to have the status of a universal protector, so that the provision of military services or equipment to forces operating under the authority of the United Nations would be likely to satisfy the criteria of protection.

BUSINESS ETHICS

BUSINESS ETHICS ARTICLES

INTRODUCTION

In 2015, I was the guest speaker at Edgware United Synagogue's Shabbat UK events. In the course of one or two of my talks over the Shabbat, I indulged my mono-mania on the subject of the poor state of business ethics within the Orthodox Jewish community compared to our punctilious observance of religious ritual.

Shortly afterwards, I was approached by someone who had been in the audience and who was involved in trying to increase the editorial content of an advertising publication that is widely distributed to Orthodox Jewish households in North West London. He asked if I would write a series of pieces about business ethics for this publication, and I agreed to do so.

My expectation at the time was that writing about practical business ethics issues such as not holding a "sale" when it is simply an advertising gimmick and the prices have not been reduced in any real sense, or accepting payments in cash, would be so provocative for the advertisers in this particular publication as well as for many of its readers that the series would be unlikely to last very long.

The first few articles received no adverse comment, possibly because nobody noticed that they were there at all: after a while, the publication did begin to receive some complaints. Oddly enough, the article that seemed to engender the most fury was when I suggested that people might like to consider ethical sourcing for animal products.

After fourteen episodes, I was told that they thought they might take a break from the business ethics content for a while and would come back to me shortly: I am not surprised not to have heard from them since...

The Talmud relates that the first question a Jewish person is asked after his or her death is whether they dealt honestly in their daily business lives. The message does not appear to have got through: as a community, it still seems to be much more important which rabbinic institution has testified to the kosher status of the products in a particular shop, then to investigate whether the owner's bankruptcy and re-emergence with the same name and similar products on sale has effectively defrauded creditors, a situation in which purchasers from the new store risk being effectively complicit whether they know about it or are simply reckless. We don't assume that meat is kosher unless it has a rabbinic certification to that effect: we should not assume that businesses are ethical unless we have also undertaken an element of due diligence.

Here are the fourteen articles (which I wrote without payment, and in which I expressly retained copyright) that I managed to get away with before finally provoking my audience into ending the series ... (I wrote an earlier series on business ethics for the Jewish Chronicle but decided not to ask for permission to reprint them, as I think all or most of the same issues are covered in the articles reproduced below.)

(1)

GOODS AND SERVICES
"ON SALE"

Advertising goods or services as being available at a special "sale" price is a tempting way of attracting additional custom. What are the Jewish ethical issues that have to be reflected in advertising a sale?

First and foremost, dina d'malchuta dina (the law of the land is part of halachah) applies in this area; so a Jewish advertiser needs to be scrupulously careful in complying with the secular consumer law on the subject. Although there is a considerable amount of technical law in this area, including European Union law and UK consumer law, a trader who uses his or her common sense is unlikely to go far wrong. In particular, you are unlikely to fall foul of the law if: (a) you have actually traded at the pre-sale price for a number of months; (b) you intend to continue trading at the pre-sale price or a higher price following the sale period; and (c) the goods and services are identical in all respects to those sold before the sale.

In addition to the rules of consumer law, Jewish traders will need to have regard to the widest implications of midvar sheker tirchok (stay well away from anything false) as a principle of Jewish business ethics. In the context of sales, this will mean attention to the use of words like "special price", "bargain", "holiday deal", "once-in-a-lifetime opportunity" and similar advertising techniques. Secular consumer law may regard these as "mere puffs" rather than as specific representations that can be controlled by law; but Jewish ethical considerations will require greater attention to avoid misleading the purchaser.

By way of example, it is misleading (and probably unlawful) to announce a "sale" where what is actually happening is that you intend to increase the price of goods or services but are postponing the increase for a certain period during which you propose to describe the original price as a "sale" price. It is also misleading to acquire inferior stock at a lower price in order to be able to sell as "sale" goods articles that are similar to, but in fact lower quality than, goods sold before the sale period, if you are hoping that people will buy in reliance on the reputation of the quality of the pre-sale goods. (There is of course nothing wrong with selling inferior goods at lower prices if people are clear that is what they are buying.)

Where a purchaser was influenced by the belief that they were taking advantage of a special sale opportunity and finds out that in fact they were buying goods or services of the normal quality at the normal price, Jewish law may provide remedies not available as a matter of English consumer law. In particular, if a Beis Din were satisfied that the purchaser would not have bought the goods or services but for the representation of a "sale", it might conclude that the purchase was a mekach to'us (deal based on mistake) and order a complete refund. As with all issues in this area, the result would depend on the precise circumstances.

(2)

PAYING IN CASH

*Service providers sometimes ask to be paid in cash:
what are the Jewish ethical issues involved in deciding
whether or not to comply with their request?*

There are various entirely legitimate and lawful reasons
why a service-provider may wish to receive some or all
of the payment for services in cash. At the same time, it
is well-known that one of the most common reasons for
traders to ask to be paid in cash is in order to conceal
part of their takings from the tax authorities, which
engages a simple Jewish prohibition of gezel min
ho'rabim (stealing from the public).

The practice of tax evasion through suppressing cash
receipts is too widespread for a customer to be able
simply to pay in cash and argue that it is entirely up to
the trader whether or not he or she takes advantage of
that form of payment to break the law. In essence, a
person who agrees to pay in cash risks being a machzik
yedei aveiro (helping someone to break the law). (They
will also quite possibly incur secular civil or criminal
liability of some kind if they are thought to have been
knowingly or recklessly conniving at tax evasion.)

This does not mean that a customer should necessarily refuse a request to pay in cash, but he or she has an obligation to establish that there is a lawful reason for the request.

For example, a caterer dealing with a function may need to pay the waiting and other catering staff on the day of the event in cash (either because they don't all have bank accounts, or because they do not qualify for free banking and wish to avoid cheque charges, or simply because they wish to be able to spend the money straight away). In such a case, there is no reason why the customer should not pay some of the costs in cash on the day of the event.

Another common and legitimate reason for a request to pay in cash is a small business' wish to avoid banking charges. Particularly in the case of relatively small payments, cheque or other credit charges for business accounts can be considerable, and there is no reason why the customer should not assist the trader in reducing overall finance costs.

The most obvious warning sign of an improper request to pay in cash is the offer of a direct or indirect discount. The legitimate business reasons discussed above for seeking cash payments might justify the offer of a small discount to reflect the increased convenience for the trader; but nothing very significant. A quote of two prices, with the cash price being significantly lower than the other is likely to indicate an intention to evade tax: in such a case, the customer should insist on a satisfactory and credible explanation of the proposed discount for cash. If an explanation is not provided, the customer must either insist on paying through a tracked-payment form at the higher price, or (depending on whether there is any uncertainty in the case) decline to deal with the supplier altogether.

Obviously, a customer who offers to pay cash in return for a substantial discount is not only being machzik yedei aveiro as stated above, but is also transgressing the Torah prohibition of lifnei iver lo titen michshol (putting an obstacle in the way of the blind – extended to tempting people to break the law generally).

(3)

WITHHOLDING RENT

If my landlord fails to maintain the flat, what are the Jewish ethical issues involved in deciding whether or not I can withhold rent?

The starting point for a Jewish ethical analysis of the issue of withholding rent is the fact that tenancy is a form of contract between the tenant and the landlord. The starting point for the Jewish ethical attitude to contracts is that both sides have in effect made promises to perform specified obligations, of which paying the rent is the primary obligation of the tenant. Aside from the fact that halachah supports the application and enforcement of the dina d'malchuta (secular law) in respect of contracts, from a purely ethical perspective the duty to perform a promise that I have made is not automatically excused by the fact that other people have failed to perform promises that they have made to me.

This notion is qualified where the promises are seen as reciprocal in intent.

It is not right for me to try to "take revenge" on someone who has broken a promise made to me, by breaking a promise that I made to him or her. The

English adage "two wrongs don't make a right" is strongly supported by the Jewish ethical notion that I am responsible for my own standards of behaviour and am not excused from behaving properly by the fact that other people may have behaved as badly or worse.

But reciprocal promises are made in the expectation (to a greater or lesser extent) that their performance is inter-dependent; and obligations under a tenancy are one of the best examples. I am paying rent in effect as the price of the provision to me of a property that can be occupied in a reasonable state of comfort – and failure to maintain the property in that state justifies me to some extent, ethically if not legally, in modifying my own obligations. In essence, the tenant's obligation to pay rent is directly related to the landlord's obligation to maintain the property: my acceptance of the obligation to pay rent rested implicitly on the expectation of performance of the landlord's obligations under the tenancy, so I am not "breaking my word" if I match performance of my obligations to the performance of the landlord's obligations.

English secular law recognises this to a certain extent. It does not in general permit tenants to withhold rent even where the landlord is in breach of obligations under the tenancy; but in certain circumstances the tenant may have the right to use money that would have been paid in rent to pay for repairs that the landlord ought to have carried out. This is a limited right, subject to taking specified procedural steps, and should not be relied on without advice, as it could lead to the tenants making themselves vulnerable to possession proceedings, whether or not the landlord should have done the work originally. But it does reflect the ethical notion that the promises in a tenancy are to some extent inter-dependent.

The halachah too supports this notion, which may become of practical relevance where the tenant and landlord are both orthodox Jews whose religious obligations require them to submit civil disputes between them to a Beis Din before taking enforcement action in the secular courts. Some tenancy agreements between orthodox Jews will stipulate for arbitration in a Beis Din in cases of conflict; while many situations will either require or permit alternative dispute resolution before resorting to legal proceedings, and a Beis Din is capable of acting as an arbitrator under the Arbitration Act 1996 (in which case its awards can be enforced through the secular law in accordance with the provision of that Act). A Beis Din will approach cases wherever possible through an approach of pesharah (compromise); and as one of the considerations to be applied for that purpose, it may explore setting off corresponding obligations between the parties. So even though the tenant owes the rent to the landlord whether or not the landlord has performed his or her obligations, a failure to maintain which has caused the tenant the financial loss entailed in carrying out work that the landlord should have done creates, in effect, a debt from the landlord to the tenant which could be set against the debt of unpaid rent.

In the climate of today's housing market, the avoidance of oppressive or extortionate practices is most obviously seen as an issue for landlords; but it is equally important for tenants, who have much of the law on their side particularly when it comes to obtaining possession of a residential property. Much as it will be clearly unethical for landlords to ignore their obligations under a lease in the knowledge that they can insist on the payment of rent independently of their own performance, so too it may be unethical for a tenant to withhold rent on the excuse of the landlords' failure to perform a minor obligation or where the landlords have clearly done everything possible to attempt to perform their obligations.

(4)

UNDER-CHARGING

Where a shop-keeper gives me too much change and I don't notice until I have left the shop, what obligations do I have as a matter of Jewish law and ethics to go back and return the money?

There is a temptation to answer by saying that of course you are always obliged as a matter of ethical behaviour, even if not by law, to return money that someone else has given you in error. But an extreme example shows that this would be too simplistic a response. Imagine that on my way back to London after a once-off visit to Manchester that I stop to buy petrol, and the sales assistant pays me 5p too much change by mistake which I don't discover until I get home: driving back up the motorway to return the 5p would clearly be more certifiable than ethical.

For the purposes of establishing the principles on which Jewish law and ethics approaches questions of this kind, we start from two basic concepts: yi'ush ba'alim (the idea that once the owner loses hope of recovering a lost object it becomes ownerless and the obligation to search for the owner in order to return it falls away) and mechilah (the concept that the person to whom a debt is owed can choose to waive it).

From these two concepts, one can establish the following principles. If the amount of money by which you have been overpaid is so large that the owner will probably notice it and would certainly hope to recover it, then you will have a Jewish legal obligation to return it (although not to spend your own money on travelling or other charges for that purpose). If the amount of money by which you have been overpaid is completely insignificant for all purposes, you can assume that the owner will not notice it, or that if he or she does notice it they will instantly write it off in their minds - in which case you have no legal or ethical obligation to return it.

As so often, therefore, the extremes are easy to identify and enunciate; but how do we navigate the grey area in between? In particular, how do we determine what amounts to a significant sum of money? A useful rule of thumb in these circumstances is that you are entitled to take as a starting point the assumption that what is insignificant to you will be insignificant to the shopkeeper. Ask yourself, if I had been over-charged by that amount rather than under-charged, would I go back to the shop to complain? If the answer is yes, then there is little doubt that you have at least an ethical duty to treat the shop-keeper as you would like to be treated yourself, and to return the extra payment. If the answer is no, then from a purely ethical perspective you may choose to ask yourself an additional question: are there reasons why what is insignificant to me might be significant to the shop-keeper? (In this context, it is as well to bear in mind that the profit-margin on some high-bulk items can be very small - a matter of 5% or less; so that an over-payment in change of 5p might amount to the entire profit element on the sale.)

It is clear that I do not have to spend my own money on restoring someone else's property that they have given to me, whether or not by mistake. If a business pays me significantly too much money by mistake I have a duty to return it - but I am entitled to deduct any expenses of doing so, including banking charges, postal costs and so on. A more difficult question is whether I am obliged to spend time on returning the over-payment, and whether I can charge for my time if I do so. Although this can be complicated both from a legal and an ethical perspective, I am entitled at the least to take into account any direct loss of earnings that I suffer as a result of taking time to restore the over-payment, and deduct the amount of that loss as if it were any other kind of direct expense incurred.

If in doubt whether the shop-owner wants me to go to the trouble of returning a relatively trivial over-payment I may be tempted to pick up the phone and check that he or she is content to grant express mechilah (waiver) for the amount. That is without doubt an ethically impressive course of action, but it requires a note of caution: if I am not speaking to the actual owner of the business, but to an employee (or even co-owner), I can rely on his or her waiver only if satisfied in the circumstances that it falls within the authority that has been delegated to them by the owner. It is famously easy to be generous with other people's money, and a cheery assurance that I don't need to worry about the over-payment is worthless unless it comes either from the person whose money it is or from someone who has clear authority to act on that person's behalf in relation to sums of that kind.

Finally, whose duty is it to check whether payments are correct or not? In law, this varies considerably; and people are sometimes surprised to learn, for example, that as a matter of both secular and Jewish law if a person makes a payment into my bank account in error it is my duty to report it, and I cannot simply take the line that if asked to return it I will but otherwise I will keep it and eventually spend it. At the other extreme, I clearly have neither a legal nor an ethical duty to check a long shopping receipt from the supermarket to satisfy myself that the assistant has not omitted an item or charged the wrong price. Where the balance is to be struck between these two extremes is again difficult to express; but as with many areas of law and ethics one has to have regard to the fifth volume of the Shulchan Aruch - the laws of common sense. In particular, if I have some reason to think that there may be a problem (most obviously, because I was expecting a bill to be larger than it is) then I have at least an ethical responsibility to check to see whether the reason is an overpayment by the shopkeeper or a miscalculation by me.

(5)

PAYING ON TIME

Not many of the 613 mitzvos are expressly dedicated to issues of business ethics, which makes it all the more surprising that the Torah deals with the issue of paying commercial debts with two separate mitzvos: the positive requirement to give a daily worker his or her wages on the day on which the work is done, and the negative prohibition of retaining wages overnight once they become due.

The parameters of these two mitzvos are relatively tight. They apply in particular to workers who are employed by the day and whose contract does not stipulate for periodic payment. So a relatively narrow range in the context of modern commerce.

But the ethical hinterland of these mitzvos encompasses a wide range of situations and issues. They remind us that we can cause serious distress and loss to people by retaining money that is due to them, and that there is little or nothing to choose from an ethical perspective between stealing money from someone and failing to pay money that I owe them. In particular, the prohibition of allowing my worker's wages to remain with me overnight is designed to remind me that the money is no longer mine.

Cleaners working for Jewish families sometimes report that their wages are regularly paid in arrears, and only after a number of requests for payment; and this occurs in some families who by outward appearances seem to wish to identify with the orthodox Jewish community. One cleaner told me that she is required to work particularly hard for one family before Pesach because the wife is extremely meticulous in cleaning her kitchen from chometz, but that she doesn't get paid for several weeks afterwards despite reminders; that family clearly need to re-balance their comparative observances of Orach Chayim and Choshen Mishpat.

Similarly, there is currently a prominent member of the orthodox Jewish community who is well-known for two things: he is known privately by his suppliers for paying bills late and only after numerous and vigorous reminders, and he is known publicly for his generosity in supporting a number of communal charities. It is this kind of unbalanced thinking that too often gives the orthodox community a bad name. On the one hand, he is happy to risk putting small traders out of business by holding back large amounts owing to them, forcing them to borrow at interest from the banks and possibly to fail to meet their financing commitments; on the other hand, once they have gone bust and are on the street, he will be happy to give them back some of the money that he should have paid them before in the form of self-righteous charitable donations. Some ethical realignment is clearly called for.

The most common situations in which ordinary people encounter this issue outside business is in the context of paying babysitters or cleaners. From a purely halachic perspective, the application of the laws of prompt payment depend in part on the express terms of any contract (oral or written) and in part on normal commercial practice, which is impliedly adopted in relation to transactions which do not make express contrary provision. So, a babysitter is clearly working on a casual part-daily basis, and will expect to be paid at the end of the session. If the family expect to allow amounts to accumulate and pay them periodically, they need to stipulate this expressly as part of the initial agreement with the babysitter.

Similarly, a cleaner is normally to be regarded as a casual day-worker and will expect to be paid at the end of each session; and if something else is intended it must be agreed at the beginning of the relationship.

Can the right to prompt payment be waived? Technically, it can: because if I owe you money and you agree that I can pay it at a later time, your agreement converts the original debt into a new loan on the terms agreed. So my obligation to pay on time is extinguished and incorporated into the debt which is now to be paid at the specified time or within the specified period. But it is dangerous to rely on this. A casual worker is likely to agree to late payment more out of fear of losing future business than because of being genuinely relaxed about when he or she receives her money; in which case, the consent to late payment is tainted or vitiated, and may not be sufficient to release me from my halachic obligation to pay on time.

There is an interesting halachic technicality that has grown up around late payment as a result of the enactment in secular English law of the Late Payment of

Commercial Debts (Interest) Act 1998. In cases to which the Act applies, late payment of the debt begins to attract statutory interest at a rate prescribed under the Act. If a Jewish business-owner orders supplies from a Jewish supplier, so the halachic prohibition against charging or paying interest on debts (ribis) applies, what is the situation in regards the statutory interest? The position is not entirely clear. There is an argument that despite being called interest the statutory payment is in the nature of a fine or penalty, which in halachic terms would be categorised as a knas and the business-owner would be obliged to pay it. But there is also an argument that the payment is interest, in which case the business-owner has a religious obligation not to pay it and the supplier has a religious obligation not to receive it. But the business-owner will have a secular obligation to pay the interest, and the ability to waive the statutory debt or to contract out of it will not always operate, depending on the circumstances. So, the only way to avoid this conundrum is to ensure that we all pay our debts as promptly as possible.

(6)

HOSPITALITY

Probably few if any business deals will be done at the
Purim Seudah – so there shouldn't be too many issues
about whether deals agreed with people who were
affected by alcohol are valid after the event! But are
there wider ethical considerations about business
hospitality?

First, don't be too sure that no business is done at
Purim Seudos! What about all the charity representatives
who come around collecting? Joking aside, they need to
be careful that if people are feeling "merry" enough to
be more than usually generous – which is very much in
the spirit of Purim – they are not so far gone as to be
incapable of thinking seriously about whether they are
genuinely happy to give away a particular sum. Taking
money from someone who is drunk – whether or not he
or she declares at the time that they are happy to donate
– could raise real issues of consent and intention after the
event, and could involve the charity in questions of avak
gezel (theft-related matters).

As to the more general issues of business hospitality,
from the Jewish ethical perspective they fall under two

broad headings: shochad (bribery) and da'as (intent to enter into legally binding relations).

As to shochad, while the Torah prohibition on bribery is primarily concerned with judicial decision-making, its halachic and ethical hinterland extends to many different kinds of discretionary function, both in public service and in commerce. (While corruption in secular law was once primarily perceived as being entirely concerned with the public service, since the passage of the Bribery Act 2010 there is a much broader understanding of the implications of corruption in private commercial settings.)

At one extreme, extravagant hospitality which is deliberately intended to obtain the goodwill of the guest, to make him or her feel personally beholden to the host and to influence the guest's commercial decisions on behalf of an employer or other third party, clearly engages questions of bribery both in law and as a matter of ethics. At the other extreme, providing modest refreshments at a business meeting to enable it to continue for a length of time or over a mealtime clearly raises no issues whether of law or of ethics. Between the two extremes there is a grey area which can be tricky to navigate, and as to which the best guide as always will be common sense. (It will, however, be important to check whether either the host or the guest organisation has rules or guidance in place which might impose more stringent requirements than common sense alone might dictate.)

In terms of Jewish ethical considerations, it should also be remembered that there is a concept of shochad lemafreya (retrospective bribery): an extravagant party thrown after the conclusion of a deal may be seen as compromising the commercial integrity of the guests, whether because it was promised or hinted at earlier on and may have influenced negotiations, or because it may be seen as an attempt to influence future relations.

The issue of daas in general, and g'neivas daas ("stealing the mind") in particular, arises wherever decisions are to be made under the influence of hospitality. It is well known, for example, that sales teams pushing timeshare or similar products often provide free alcohol in the knowledge that potential customers become less critical and careful even when far from being drunk or anything like it. To put it at its lowest, this is introducing an irrelevant factor into the negotiations, trying to soften the customer's critical faculties, and any self-respecting business would avoid the use of tactics of this kind. However, there will sometimes be a fine line between the use of alcohol or other entertainment to encourage guests to make deals which they would not otherwise make, and providing a congenial business environment in which guests can relax and make sensible unpressurised decisions. Again, the key guiding factors will be common sense and the relevant industrial norms of behaviour, qualified only by any particularly stringent rules or guidance operated by the particular host or guest organisations.

It occasionally occurs that a guest at an event at an occasion at which alcohol is served over-indulges, when that was far from the intention of the organisers of the event, and is no longer in a position to make sensible commercial decisions. It goes without saying that businesses and individual entrepreneurs will have their own rules designed to ensure firstly that guests are not encouraged to over-indulge and, secondly, that no unfair advantage is taken of any guest who happens to become "merrier" than is appropriate on any day except Purim!

(7)

TRADING BY CHARITIES

A number of Jewish charities now undertake trading in various ways, including running shops for unwanted goods and providing a range of other commercial services, often at very attractive prices: I have always assumed that it must be a good thing to use charities for services wherever possible, but perhaps it's not always quite so simple?

The starting point for this topic from the Jewish business ethics perspective is that it is always excellent when charities go beyond simply asking people for donations, and start to engage in activities that help those involved in the charity in other and more permanent ways. The Jewish concept of charitable giving is encapsulated in the Torah's phrase "v'hechzakto bo" ("you should strengthen him") – the highest aim of the Jewish concept of tzedoko is not to give people money but to help them to become self-reliant.

So, it is great to see charities harnessing the energies and enthusiasm of their beneficiaries to provide services on commercial or semi-commercial terms, so that they are not simply receiving donations but are learning and practising skills that both make them feel self-reliant in the short-term and may help them to become actually self-reliant in the long-term.

But yes, there is another side to this as well. Charities necessarily trade on advantageous terms, because of their nature and natural advantages. A service-provider set up on charitable premises may be paying no rent at all, because the charity subsidises its subsidiary commercial venture; or it may be paying rent but at a lower than arms-length commercial rate. And it may be able to take advantage of the charity's position in a number of other ways, ranging from economies of scale in ordering supplies to simply relying on the goodwill attaching to the charity's name to attract clients. That inevitably amounts to a distortion of the market-place, and charities need to take great care to ensure that the distortion is not significantly to the detriment of other traders who deserve to operate on an equal playing-field in order to survive.

To apply this in practice, take the following examples (each of which is purely theoretical and is not based on any past or present actual example known to the author).

Start with second-hand shops run by charities. In general, they are probably seen as an asset to the high street by neighbouring businesses, as another way of attracting potential customers to the area. And they are not for the most part in direct competition with their neighbours. But they might wish to think about the range of products they stock to ensure that they remain complementary to and not a threat to surrounding businesses. A good example might be second hand school uniform: as a purely theoretical example, if a charity shop started to stock second hand school uniforms that might be a fantastic service for the local community; but depending on the scale of the enterprise it could also come in practice to threaten the margins of local special-ist school uniform suppliers, either driving up prices for those using their services or potentially threatening their viability. Obviously, it is all a matter of fact and degree; but it simply deserves thought by those determining the range of products to accept for resale.

As to the provision of services, again one needs to take a broad view of the potential ethical consider-ations. Imagine a charity set up to relive poverty among local residents which decides to provide pest control services to the local area, taking advantage of its good name, and premises and vehicles supplied at low cost by the charity. This could have a fantastic impact on the lives of the volunteers or workers who operate the service. But the pest-control field is a relatively small field, and the service could quickly have an impact on the viability of local traders who specialise in that area. Nothing is served by a charity founded to relieve poverty doing so by putting local traders out of business and into poverty!

Similar considerations apply to the sale of groceries or other commodities at discounted prices. Again, superficially a wholly beneficial activity for a charity which aims to relieve poverty, and one whose effects can only be positive; instead of being made to feel like the recipients of charitable donations, beneficiaries are able to shop like anyone else, in the knowledge that the prices are kept down because the charity does not need to make a profit. But what about the local traders who do need to make a profit? Again, in the sales industry margins can be tight and profit-loss balances fragile. In a small community-based area it would be possible to have a significant impact on prices in a relatively short time, and the result could be to undermine the viability of local retail businesses. Charities would need to ask themselves careful questions about the potential effect of their retail activities on other businesses before being able to be satisfied that the overall effect of their activities was positive. While they might decide that lowering prices would be in the interests of consumers anyway, that is not always the case: if retailers are presently profiteering in reliance on a monopoly situation, for example, then exerting pressure on their margins can be only a good thing; but if they are holding a difficult balance between profit and loss, squeezing margins further could undermine them and put them out of business altogether, which is not only bad for them but potentially disadvantageous for consumers in the longer term.

So, charity trading is as complicated as every other issue in business ethics; and those charities who offer commercial services, and those people who choose to take advantage of them, need to consider the broader implications before deciding what services to offer, and how and when to take advantage of them.

(8)

FUR

Fur is back in fashion: what do Jewish law and ethics have to say about it?

In principle, there is no halachic or ethical objection to the wearing of fur. Rather the contrary: classic Jewish sources embrace the idea that animals were created to be of use to humans, and that they somehow achieve their potential by contributing to our happiness and comfort. At the same time, there is a strong notion of kvod habrios (respect for all creations) that gives rise to specific halachic obligations to avoid tzaar baalei chaim (cruelty to animals).

As a matter of strict halachah, I have in general no obligation to investigate the source of animal products that are sold to me from a perspective of ensuring that the animals have been treated correctly (particularly because in the case of slaughtered meat the laws of shechitah incorporate protection for animal welfare to a high degree).

But there is a difference between having a duty to inquire into the origin of animal products and the treatment of the animals, and deliberately shutting one's eyes to animal cruelty that one either does know about or would naturally suspect if one turned one's mind to the question. In the case of hunted fur, there is no particular reason to suspect cruelty; it is true that traps are sometimes used as well as straight shooting, but there is naturally a premium on shot fur as the pelt is less likely to be damaged, and so as a general rule one may be able to assume that high-quality hunted fur products are produced relatively humanely.

The resurgence of the fashion for fur, however, and the recent demand for it as a low-cost fashion product, has concentrated the industry on farmed rather than hunted fur. And the economics of fur farming are obviously based on tightening margins rather than setting standards for animal welfare. A number of fur-producing animals are presently kept (both in European and non-European settings) in conditions that would definitely offend against Jewish principles of tzaar baalei chaim; and for farmed animals gassing is still a painful and common method of slaughter so as to avoid damaging the pelt. Indeed, when one considers the price of certain fur products in clothing stores today and asks oneself how they could be produced for the price, a reasonably sensitive shopper is likely to suspect that the animals are likely to be maintained and killed in unpleasant conditions.

While this certainly does not translate into a clear halachic prohibition against buying fur without investigating the conditions in which the animals producing it are kept, those whose Jewish life goes beyond avoiding technical prohibitions and includes embracing and applying underlying principles of Jewish ethics are likely to feel a responsibility to think about the processes by which fur (and other animal products) are put on the market.

This might have been asking rather a lot of the average consumer a few years ago: today, however, when the general market-place includes a range of sectors committed to animal welfare and other ethical principles, it should not be difficult for a Jewish consumer to find ways of ensuring that fur comes from animals kept in conditions compatible with Jewish principles of animal welfare.

The idea that "they'll sell it anyway whether I buy it or not" is not, of course, in accordance with Jewish ethical teaching. Avoiding being machzik yedei ovrei aveirah (supporting wrong-doers) is a fundamental Jewish principle; and we know that consumers today can quickly and significantly influence market conditions by their buying patterns, particularly if they take the trouble to express the ethical and other matters that affect their choice of produce.

Of particular relevance to the orthodox Jewish community is the fact that the hats which men wear are mostly sourced from naturally produced felt, which is an animal product. Synthetic versions do exist (and are now in common use for Chassidish shtreimlech for example) but most common brands are natural felt. Buyers who wish to regard themselves as sensitive to Jewish ethical principles of cruelty to animals are therefore likely to wish to inquire of makers and sellers where they source their materials or products, and what they are able to tell the consumer about the conditions in which any farmed rabbits or other felt-producing animals are kept.

Fake fur is of course sold extensively today. There was at one time a sentiment against it, when there was a general prejudice against fur clothes generally, based partly on animal welfare considerations. Today, with fur returning to fashion generally, the availability of fake fur is such that most people are likely to consider it neither insensitive in itself nor to be avoided for other ethical reasons. (And the wide availability of fake fur means that most consumers will probably not worry that people might think they are wearing real fur, despite the realism of some of the better synthetic brands.)

Finally, it should be noted that although vegetarianism and veganism have not traditionally been mainstream within the orthodox Jewish communities, there have always been those whose sensitivity to the feelings of animals as an aspect of their kvod habrios has led them to avoid the use of animal products entirely or to a certain extent. They are likely to regard fur as an unnecessary fashion accessory rarely produced without any cruelty to animals, and therefore best avoided; and their view is entitled to respect from an ethical perspective, whether or not one shares it.

(9)

DISCOUNT VOUCHERS

There is a local shop that allows you to use discount vouchers for products that they stock against the cost of your overall shopping, whether or not you actually bought the product named in the voucher. What are the Jewish business ethical implications?

This is such a straight forward question that it is surprising that it arises so often. Perhaps understandably, shoppers are anxious to make as full use of discount vouchers as possible and this sometimes appears to cloud their judgement on what would otherwise be a straight forward issue.

A discount voucher is simply a form of contractual arrangement between the manufacturer or wholesaler of a particular product and the consumer or retailer (or both). The terms of the contract are extremely simple: if you buy the specified product in accordance with any timing or other conditions specified on the voucher then the manufacturer or wholesaler will pay you a specified proportion of the purchase price, or will ask the retailer to lower the price and then reimburse the retailer.

When the retailer returns the vouchers to the manufacturer or wholesaler they require an express or implied warrantee that the conditions set out in the vouchers have been satisfied. Clearly, the most important of those conditions is that on each occasion when the voucher was used the specified product was purchased. Each time a retailer returns the voucher to the manufacturer without having sold the product, the retailer is simply stealing a (normally) tiny amount of money from the manufacturer or wholesaler.

That this is a simple case of theft is easy to demonstrate. If the retailer were to say to the manufacturer openly, "I did not sell any of your products but I would like you to give me money in exchange for this voucher" the answer would of course be no. Obtaining the money on the express or implied pretence that the voucher was accepted against the purchase of one of the manufacturer's products is therefore simply obtaining money on false pretences or, in common parlance, stealing.

Strictly speaking, the theft is being carried out by the retailer and not by the consumer in the case described above. As a matter of secular law, the consumer may well be committing the offence of encouraging or assisting the retailer to obtain money on false pretences. In Jewish ethical terms, in any event, the consumer who presents the voucher to the retailer in circumstances where they both know that the conditions of the voucher have not been satisfied is being machzik yedei ovrei aveiro (assisting wrongdoers) which is in itself a very serious prohibition.

The fact that this is such a prevalent practice is simply evidence that consumers' thinking so easily becomes a little muddled where their own financial interests are concerned. For example, I have heard the excuse that the retailer only accepts the vouchers in cases where the product is stocked in the store "so I could have bought it if I wanted to". Quite clearly this is irrelevant: in legal and ethical terms, it is no different from shoplifting and arguing that "I had the money in my pocket so I could have paid if I wanted to".

Any other instance of attempting to use a voucher outside its strict terms and conditions raises precisely the same legal and ethical considerations. For example, using or accepting an out of date voucher is a clear case of theft, although in this case it is more likely to be theft from the retailer by the consumer than from the manufacturer by the retailer. Either way, whether the voucher will be dishonoured by the manufacturer when the retailer presents it and he or she will therefore be out of pocket, or whether the retailer will be able to pretend that it was accepted within the stated time, the consumer will have effectively stolen the money, whether from the retailer or from the manufacturer through the retailer.

Of course, we are talking generally about tiny amounts of money for discount vouchers. The halachic de minimis threshold for theft is very low, amounting to the smallest amount of money that a person would consider significant. In today's accounting terms for manufacturers and retailers, profit margins are often so tight that what might appear to be an insignificant amount in relation to a single transaction becomes significant when looked at as a market trend; and the assumption that a person does not care about losing less than a shoveh prutah ceases to apply when manufacturers or retailers are looking at their books overall rather than at the amounts on individual transactions.

In any event, Jewish ethical behaviour demands more of people than simply avoiding committing technical halachic or secular prohibitions and offences; and those who wish to translate their observance of Shulchan Aruch into an overall ethical approach to life, will not wish to benefit even below a de minimis threshold from misuse of discount vouchers.

(10)

BREAKAGES IN SHOPS

My child knocked over a glass dish in a shop the other day and the shopkeeper tried to make me pay for it (which I refused to do): whom do Jewish business ethics support in this case, me or the shop-keeper?

You will not be surprised to hear that the answer depends on the precise circumstances.

Secular legal liability generally depends on establishing a basis for responsibility, arising from a contract or from the negligence or other wrong-doing of one side or the other. As a general rule, without fault of some kind or a contractual or other legal assumption of responsibility, there will be no secular legal liability.

The halachah takes account of contractual responsibility and of the presence or absence of negligence; but they are not necessarily the determining factors. In the classic Biblical case of a no-fault accident between two items of property in the course of which one is damaged and the other is not (oxen, in the text, but they could just as well be motor-cars) the financial burden of the accident is in effect shared, rather than one person bearing the entire burden just because his or her property happened to be stronger on the day. In other contexts, the halachah is as rigidly fault-based as in secular law, and the maxim "the person who wants to extract money from someone else is the one who has to prove the liability" is applied. In other contexts, there is in effect a halachic presumption of fault without proof being necessary: the most obvious example being the borrower's liability for no-fault damage.

The most obvious question in this case will be "whose fault was it?", looking at all the circumstances. For example, piling dishes in stacks right on the edge of shelves may be making it almost impossible to avoid incidents of this kind (more so if this is a shop where children are expected or encouraged). At the other end of the spectrum, taking children into a shop selling only high-value and fragile articles, is asking for trouble. Which of these two extremes is your case nearer? You may also wish to ask yourself whether your child was having an occasional "off-day" or behaved entirely normally and reasonably.

Some shops have notices up to the effect that breakages must be paid for. Whether those are legally effective will depend in part on whether they are presented with sufficient prominence, and in such a way, as to be clearly requiring an acceptance of responsibility by those who choose to enter the shop. It will also be relevant whether and how the article was handled: no notice of this kind will be sufficient to pass to the customer liability for an article which simply falls apart when examined before purchase in the normal manner.

An additional legal and halachic issue that arises in your case is whether you are responsible for liabilities incurred by your child. Again, depending on the precise circumstances, it will sometimes be possible both in secular law and in halachah to disclaim liability for your children's behaviour; but it is not always an attractive position to adopt (or one that will play an effective part in building our children's sense of personal moral responsibility – although requiring a contribution from pocket-money might well be part of that process!).

The application of these halachic principles will inevitably produce anomalies, as hard-letter law always does. It is one of the functions of Jewish business ethics to pick up where the strict halachah leaves off, and to suggest areas where people may choose to act lifnim mishuras hadin (over and above the legal requirements). For example, if you decide that you are not responsible for the damage you might choose to pay if the price of the dish is trivial for you but may be more significant to the shop-keeper; or you might wish to protect the person who filled the shelf carelessly from the anger of the shop-owner, by paying for the breakage but offering a friendly word of advice at the same time about stacking shelves in the future.

You and the shopkeeper may think it worth referring this case to a beis din. Batei din are required to pursue compromise before delivering a halachic ruling (in which respect the rabbis anticipated the modern fashion for alternative dispute resolution by a millennium or two). A skillful beis din should be able propose a solution which both sides will consider fair in the light of all the circumstances.

(11)

COMPARATIVE ADVERTISING

I want to advertise my business by telling people how much cheaper I am than the other services in the area: I am told that comparative advertising is permitted as a matter of secular law, but what about Jewish business law and ethics?

The secular law in relation to comparative advertising can be complicated, and is necessarily fact-specific; but you are right to say that as a general rule there is no secular legal objection to drawing attention to prices or other features of competitors' businesses in order to illustrate the attractions of one's own.

Leaving aside possible complications in relation to the use of competitors' trademarks – which are unlikely to arise in relation to small or medium-sized neighbourhood businesses – the principles determining the lawfulness of comparative advertising are primarily set by European Directive 2006/114/EC (Misleading and Comparative Advertising Directive). Article 4 imposes requirements for comparative advertisements broadly along the following lines: they must not mislead; they must compare goods or services intended for the same purpose; they must compare by reference to relevant, verifiable and representative features (which may include price); they may not discredit or denigrate competitors' products or services; they must not take unfair advantage of the reputation of a trade mark or present products or services as being imitations or replicas of protected products or services; and they must not create confusion.

Interestingly, these principles cover much the same ground as the relevant Jewish ethical principles. In particular, there are two main issues that arise in relation to comparative advertising from a Jewish perspective.

First, there is the prohibition against g'neivas da'as (literally – "stealing the mind"; figuratively – misleading people). Provided that comparative advertising is designed to clarify genuine differences between you and your competitors, it is in the interests of consumers, making it easier for them to make purchasing decisions, and is in accordance with and encouraged by the principles of Jewish business ethics. As soon as it becomes an attempt to deceive or mislead, it is simply prohibited.

To give a simple example, if you and your competitor sell precisely the same product produced by the same manufacturer, and you charge significantly less than your competitor, then there is no objection to your promoting your business by drawing the public's attention to the difference. There may, of course, be entirely justifiable personal or commercial reasons why your competitors feel obliged to charge more than you do, but that need not inhibit you from inviting consumers to make purchasing decisions on the basis of price, and giving them the necessary information for that purpose. But if you sell a product that is (or might be thought to be) inferior or simply different in quality to a product sold by your competitor, you must be very particular not to advertise the two products in such a way as might encourage a prospective customer to make a direct comparison between two prices as if the quality were identical. To put it simply, both legal and ethical principles require you to compare like with like, and to be scrupulous in doing so by considering all features of the two products or services that might be considered relevant to a consumer.

The halachic equivalent of the secular requirement not to discredit or denigrate competitors' products or services is the law of loshon horo (broadly, defamation). The laws of loshon horo are complex and technical, but in the context of providing business information for prospective consumers the broad principles are again similar to those set out in the European Directive. The laws of loshon horo do not prevent me from telling people things that they might want or need to know in the context of commerce; and I am positively encouraged to tell people facts that may help them to avoid making unwise business decisions. So, if I believe that people are paying higher prices than they need to by going to my competitors, there is no reason why I should not tell people the facts so they can make an informed consumer choice.

Once again, however, the emphasis is on the word "facts". I need to be absolutely sure that I am not including in my advertisement anything that is inaccurate or might be misleading. For example, if I choose to advertise a price differential, as well as ensuring like-for-like in relation to the product or service, if my price is a promotional discount or conditional on purchasing a number of products or in any other way anything other than my standard price, I must make sure that the advertisement is absolutely clear on the point.

In summary, the principles of Jewish business ethics support anything that enhances consumer understanding of the market-place and may prevent exploitation of consumers by empowering them to make discerning purchasing decisions. But those decisions must be based on facts that are accurate and that avoid anything that is or might be misleading.

(12)

CHARITY GAMBLING

Charity lotteries seem to be becoming more frequent, with higher-value tickets and prizes: what do Jewish law and ethics have to say about this trend?

The Talmud discusses two possible reasons for the disqualification of habitual gamblers as witnesses and judges in a Jewish court. The first objection is that gambling may raise issues of quasi-theft, since at the time when the gambler places the stake he or she does not really intend to lose the money, and is actuated primarily by the hope that they will win. The second objection is that someone whose income derives from gambling is not playing a useful part in the social order and doesn't have a clear picture of commercial and economic realities for working people.

It is the first of these objections that is most relevant to the use of gambling as a fund-raising tool for charities. Clearly, a traditional raffle where the tickets are perhaps a pound each and the prizes are relatively trivial, raises no serious issues on the quasi-theft side: people participate in raffles of this kind out of goodwill towards the charity, they put down some small-change without any qualms that they might not see any return, and if they win the bottle of wine, hamper or travel-ticket it simply comes as a pleasant surprise. But the same cannot be said of a lottery where the tickets are £20 a time or more, with encouragement to stake very significant sums of money based on reduced prices for multiple tickets, and with prizes worth several thousands of pounds. There is a real chance that people are participating in these lotteries on the basis of a calculated hope that they will win, in which case the Talmudic objection based on asmachta (conditional deal) would apply and raise issues of quasi-theft.

Clearly Jewish charities will wish to be certain of avoiding any possible issue of mitzvah habo ba'aveiro (mitzvo brought about by a prohibition) and will therefore be anxious that their fund-raising income should be free from any possible taint of quasi-theft. They will therefore wish to avoid any fund-raising lottery where the prize values may be exerting an influence on participants' decisions so that they pay money that they are not genuinely happy to lose to the charity, and which even a small part of their mind is happy to risk only because of a false expectation of winning.

This is the key Jewish ethical issue that arises in relation to charity lotteries; but there are others too. A number of advertisements for charity lotteries with high-value tickets carry an announcement that people may pay for their tickets out of ma'aser money. Without discussing the justification for the ruling that ma'aser money may be used in a situation where a person obtains the benefit of a chance to win a large amount of money (without the hope of which he or she would not part with their money), it might be thought that this answers the objection based on quasi-theft: if I am paying out of money that I am anyway obliged to give to charity, perhaps it can be said that I am happy to risk the stake-money without any expectation that I will see a return, on the grounds that I have to give the money away anyway.

That might answer the first objection, but it creates a new one: it means that charities are competing against each other by encouraging people to decide how to distribute their ma'aser money not on the basis of the halachic and ethical considerations of priorities (including, but not limited to, priority for local charities) but on the basis of which charity offers the highest-value prizes to be won. That clearly risks introducing a distracting element into what should be a halachic decision of how to apportion one's charity funds, and should be avoided by charities for that reason alone.

Competition between charities apart, it is open to question whether charities should be introducing a distracting element into the mitzvah of giving to charity: by offering significant prizes charities are encouraging the Jewish public to make decisions partly based on greed and expectation, instead of based on a pure intention to share the blessings which Hashem has given us with deserving causes.

More significantly, charities need to remind themselves that of the social evils prevalent in today's society, gambling is one of the most insidious and dangerous, responsible for destroying families and lives in ever-increasing numbers. Jewish institutions should be leading the way in reinforcing the Jewish ethical objections to gambling; they should not be encouraging young people, in particular, to become more comfortable with a concept that is one of the most destructive forces confronting today's youth. That alone should be a sufficient reason why charities might wish to think twice before running promotions that might appear to emulate some of the most seductive advertising techniques of the gambling industry and that might have a tendency to make gambling seem more acceptable within the community.

(13)

TIPS IN RESTAURANTS

I do casual work in a kosher restaurant. The restaurant charges a 12.5% service charge but quite often customers leave cash tips as well. The owner insists that she can keep the tips, because she takes them into account when calculating how much she can afford to pay the staff. What do Jewish business ethics have to say about this?

This doesn't sound like a kosher restaurant to me, unless we consider only Yoreh Deah (the part of the Shulchan Aruch – Code of Jewish Law – dealing with ritual matters) and exclude Choshen Mishpat (the part dealing with business matters)!

There could be some secular law involved here, and you may want to do some research in one of the publications that tell you about your rights, or consult a Citizens Advice Bureau. In particular, if the restaurant owner is paying you only the national minimum wage, then it is against the law for her to use customer tips to make up the amounts that she is obliged to pay you by law. There is also a Government Code of Practice about the use of tips in restaurants, which is not binding as a matter of law but is generally regarded as setting out the accepted industry standards on these matters.

The Code of Practice is also relevant to the Jewish business ethical approach to the issue, because as with many aspects of commercial halachah, a great deal depends on the minhag hamakom (accepted local custom and practice). The Code has been endorsed by a range of organisations within the service and hospitality industries, and was prepared as a result of consultation with those industries. A Beth Din, in determining what is acceptable from a halachic point of view, is likely to regard the Code as the starting point for determining standard industry practice. It could be overridden in a particular case by a clear contrary statement in a contract of employment, but if there is no written or oral term of your contract that expressly covers the point, then the minhag hamakom will become relevant and the Code of Practice will therefore acquire halachic influence.

Interestingly, the fundamental principle of the Code of Practice amounts to the same principle that would be applied by the halachah in determining what is in accordance with Jewish law, and by Jewish business ethical practice in determining what is morally acceptable behaviour. That principle is transparency: both in terms of the relationship between the restaurant and its employees and between the restaurant and its customers.

If I leave a discretionary tip in a restaurant I am intending to reward good service by the waiter or waitress who has looked after me, and my presumption is that they will be allowed to keep it. That is going to be particularly the case in a restaurant which, as you say yours does, already charges a "service charge" as part of the bill. Like many people, I assume that if I have paid an amount for service in the bill, then I do not as a general rule need to leave a tip at all; and if I do so, it is because I have received exceptional waiting service and want to show my gratitude.

By simply taking the tips for herself, your employer is therefore, to put it at the very least, risking appropriating money that has been in effect given by diners to you. That may or may not amount to actual gezel (theft) in halachah, depending on the precise circumstances, but it is certainly uncomfortably close to avak gezel (quasi-theft).

There are two actions I would expect your employer to take if she wants her restaurant to be regarded as kosher in all senses of the term.

First, she needs to ensure transparency. She needs to display in a prominent place a notice declaring that cash tips will be treated as given to the restaurant, and not to its employees. (Restaurants quite often operate a system of pooling staff tips and dividing them equally among all staff – which helps to avoid unfairness caused by "the luck of the draw" in who happens to serve generous clients: your employer will therefore need to make her notice clear enough to make people realise that it is not simply that tips are not treated as given to particular employees, but that they are not treated as given to the employees at all.) The notice should also explain what happens to the standard service charge.

Your employer is likely to be reluctant to display a notice of that kind. It is likely to lose custom (it would certainly lose mine) and does not present the restaurant in a particularly good light. That perhaps shows that in an uncertain area like business ethics, one of the best tests of ethical behaviour is not to do anything that you would be embarrassed for people to find out about!

The second action that I would expect your employer to take if she persists in appropriating money left by way of tips, is to ask a sha'aloh of a rabbi with expertise in Jewish business law. You and your colleagues should be given an opportunity to contribute to the terms in which the sha'aloh is asked; and the answer should be shared with you, preferably in writing.

Hopefully, your employer will decide to change her practice and ensure that tips are given to staff. If she does, remember that tips must be treated for tax purposes (although not for minimum wage purposes) as part of your income, and declared to HMRC annually (unless a pooling and sharing system is used in which case tax will be deducted at source).

(14)

CURRENCY FLUCTUATIONS

I ordered a new sheitel from Israel some months ago to be delivered in time for Yom Tov; the seller contacted me last week to say that it has arrived but that it will cost around 10% more because of the recent drop in the value of Sterling. What are the Jewish business law and ethics implications?

There are a number of possible issues that arise in this situation. The starting point, however, as always, is simply the terms of any contract. If you had a written contract with terms of service provided to you at the time when you agreed to buy the sheitel,[26] and those terms specified a price, then that is the price which the seller and buyer are both bound by contract to honour. If the price is expressed in Sterling then that is the end of the matter and the seller cannot now force you to pay any more. If the price is expressed in Shekalim then you cannot now object to paying the higher exchange rate.

---

[26] Form of wig worn by some orthodox Jewish married women by way of covering their own hair.

Similarly, if the price was expressed to be in Sterling but expressly subject to exchange rate fluctuations, then again you cannot object to paying the higher price.

If there was no formal document provided to you when you ordered the sheitel, it could be that as a matter of law you did not enter into a contract to buy it at all at that point, and that you are entitled now simply to back away and refuse to buy at the higher price. That would not, of course, allow you to insist on buying at the originally quoted price, but it would allow you to avoid paying the increased price.

If you signed an order form of some kind which included a reference to the seller's standard terms and conditions, the position in law and as a matter of business ethics is likely to depend both on whether those terms and conditions were made available to you at the time, and how easy it was to access them; and on whether the terms and conditions are thought to be reasonable, in the sense of striking a fair balance between the interests of the buyer and seller, or whether they are perceived as creating an unfair balance in favour of the seller.

Clearly there is straightforward consumer law involved here and you may wish to take advice, perhaps from a citizen's advice bureau or similar organisation, as to your secular legal rights. And those rights are likely to be given effect as a matter of Jewish law, given that this was a standard consumer transaction undertaken in the United Kingdom. (unless, of course, the order form you signed was actually with an Israeli supplier, and the seller here was no more than an agent).

As to the ethics of the situation, a great deal depends again on all the circumstances of the sale and the natural expectations that would be created in those circumstances. Clearly, an experienced commercial supplier would be expected to take appropriate steps to protect themselves against the possible fluctuation of exchange rates when supplying a product sourced from another country, and having quoted a price to a UK consumer in pounds Sterling, the seller might be expected as a matter of business ethics to stick to it. On the other hand, a small business with relatively little exposure to complicated commercial business might be thought to be less likely to be able to protect themselves, and it might be thought more fair for the risk, and the burden, to be shared between the two sides.

On its face, this situation sounds like something that might be worth taking to a competent and respected Beis Din, and relying upon their natural tendency to strike a pesharah (compromise) in the light of all the circumstances. At one extreme, if they were satisfied that you signed a clear contract with a price linked to the rate of exchange in some way or another, they may feel that the ethical result is for you to pay the full increased price (particularly if that also is in accordance with your strict legal obligations). At the other extreme, if they feel that the seller clearly contracted to supply at a UK price and knowingly and reasonably took the risk of currency fluctuations, they may feel that the seller must simply perform his or her obligations under the contract. If the case falls somewhere in the middle, for any of a possible wide variety of reasons, the Beis Din, or indeed a secular arbitrator, might feel that the risk should be shared somewhere along the line, and that a compromise price somewhere between the original Sterling price quoted and the new exchange equivalent should be paid.

GLOSSARY

(Note that in this glossary the ashkenazi spelling is used – the sephardi variant will sometimes be found in the articles. So, for example, Beis Din is the equivalent of Beit Din, and Shabbos is the equivalent of Shabbat.)

Ashkenazi	–	The Jewish community that came from, mostly, Germany, Poland and Russia
Beis Din	–	Rabbinic Court, dealing with ritual matters (including kashrus certification and geirus) and monetary disputes
Bamidbar	–	Hebrew for Numbers, fourth book of the Bible
Bereishis	–	Hebrew for Genesis, first book of the Bible
Botei Din	–	Plural of Beis Din
Brachah	–	Blessing (before or after food, or on certain other occasions)
Challah	–	Loaves of bread eaten at the Shabbat meals
Chareidim	–	So called "ultra-orthodox" Jews
Chassidim	–	One kind of chareidim
Chumrah	–	Halachic stringency
Dayan	–	Member of Beis Din

Dayonim	–	Plural of Dayan
Devorim	–	Hebrew for Deuteronomy, fifth book of the Bible
Eruv	–	A symbolic construction allowing orthodox Jews to carry on Shabbo
Geirus	–	Conversion to Judaism
Get	–	Jewish religious divorce
Gemara	–	Part of the Talmud (*q.v.*)
Gittin	–	Name of a Talmudic tractate
Halacha	–	Jewish law
Kashrut	–	System of regulating kosher and non-kosher food
Kehillo	–	Congregation
Kiddush	–	A Shabbat and festival ceremony normally involving a cup of wine
Kosher	–	Able to be eaten in accordance with Jewish ritual law
Matzah	–	Unleavened bread eaten at the Passover festival
Minhag	–	Custom
Mishneh	–	Part of the Talmud (*q.v.*)
Mitzvah	–	Commandment (either of Bible or developed by Rabbis)
Mitzvos	–	Plural of Mitzvah
Moschiach	–	The Messiah
Neshomoh	–	Soul
Parashah	–	Torah reading of the week
Pesach	–	Passover – a Jewish festival
Rabbi	–	Jewish religious leader

Rabbonim	–	Plural of rabbi
Rambam	–	Moses Maimonides; a medieval codifier of Jewish law
Rebbe	–	The rabbi of a Chassidic community
Seder	–	The festive meal which begins the Passover festival
Sefardi	–	The Jewish community that came mostly from Spain, Portugal and the middle East
Semichah	–	Rabbinic ordination
Seudah	–	Meal, often festive / ceremonial
Shabbos	–	The Jewish Sabbath – which starts at dusk on Friday evening and ends with nightfall on Saturday night
Shemos	–	Hebrew for Exodus, second book of the Bible
Shul	–	Synagogue
Talmud	–	A series of tractates dealing with technical aspects of Jewish law
Torah	–	The Hebrew name for the Bible
Treif	–	Not kosher
Tzedokoh	–	Charitable donations
Tzibbur	–	Congregation
Vayikra	–	Hebrew for Leviticus, third book of the Bible

Lightning Source UK Ltd.
Milton Keynes UK
UKHW01f1002110618
324047UK00001B/8/P

9 781786 239785